April 13, 2005

For Debbie - To creating wonderful memories
around family, friends and food.

Enjoy!

Catherine Fliegel

The One-Armed Cook ™

Cynthia Stevens Graubart

by Cynthia Stevens Graubart
and Catherine Fliegel, R.N., C.C.E.

Catherine Fliegel

EMPIRE PRESS Atlanta, Georgia

Library of Congress Control Number 2004090897

ISBN 0-9749045-0-3

Quantity discounts are available on bulk purchases of this book
for educational, gift purposes, or as premiums.
Special books or book excerpts can also be created to fit specific needs.
Please contact Empire Press
at empirepress@bellsouth.net for more information.

Printed and bound in the United States of America.

First Edition
1 2 3 4 5 6 7 8 9 0

Visit us at
www.theonearmedcook.com

Printed by Wimmer Cookbooks

To Dad,
I'm so glad the apple
didn't fall too far from the tree.
Love, Cynthia

For my mom, Sue Ann Voelker,
who taught me to cook and to mother from my heart.
Love, Catherine

Acknowledgments

From Cynthia

I did not come from a family of cooks. My mother, and even her mother, considered cooking a terrible chore. My sister Phylecia and I were taught at an early age to make acceptable meals of spaghetti, meatloaf, and can-of-soup casseroles to be ready when Mom came home from work. Learning to be independent in this world is so vital, and I thank you, Mom, for preparing me to take care of myself.

After college, I began my career as a television producer. I teamed up with Nathalie Dupree to help her launch her television career. Nathalie changed my culinary life, showing me how to express myself through the food I served and how to be a gracious, and organized, hostess. The roots of this book are from my precious years spent with Nathalie cooking at her side, testing recipes, writing scripts, taping television shows, traveling to learn about food, and eating many wonderful meals together. Thank you, Nathalie, for creating everlasting memories.

My husband gently reminded me over the years that I had a book in me and needed to get it out. Thank you, Cliff, for your love and support.

One summer in Maine, I was in despair regarding my life's path and over a simple lobster salad and a glass of wine, my dear friend Anne Rivers Siddons said to just be still and listen and my direction would be revealed. I did and it was. Thank you, Annie, for your endless love, generosity, and support.

Although the writing came easily to me, the project became overwhelming with many distractions along the way. I asked my friend Catherine to join me, so that I would have a partner to answer to and help me keep to my deadlines. Thank you, Catherine, for saying yes. You have been the perfect partner.

So many important people in my life have participated in this project. To my friends and family from near and far, thank you from the bottom of my heart.

Finally, to Norman and Rachel, my amazing and wonderful children: because you loved being held on my hip, we made many meals together and I thank you both for being the inspiration for this book.

To all mothers everywhere who struggle to do the best for their families: I understand how hard it is to be all things to all people. This book will help make at least a couple of hours of your day a little easier.

Cynthia Stevens Graubart

iv

From Catherine

My decision to exchange full-time jobs from hospital to home came naturally. I traded in my nursing uniforms for nursing bras and direct deposits into my checking account for direct involvement with my children. I gave up my professional identity for always being referred to as somebody's mommy. For the most part, I have never looked back. But I know that somewhere deep inside me, buried beneath the higher purpose of staying home to raise my children, there is a highly motivated career woman.

My family is my greatest passion in life. Cooking runs a close second. And while the two come together rather creatively on a daily basis, it seemed inevitable that they should merge on a more open forum. This book is the union of my true loves.

I grew up in the kitchens of my two best role models, always watching, always learning. There were no cookbooks in our home; ingredients were measured by hand and by eye and by taste. Thank you, Honey and Mom, for lending me years of your instinctive cooking and for creating wonderful memories around food and family.

After I left home and entered nursing school, I met an aspiring MBA student. In exchange for typing my term papers, I cooked for him several times a week. By my senior year, diamond ring on my finger but still desiring very much to impress this young man, I read *Gourmet Magazine* regularly and broadly expanded my cooking repertoire. Thank you, Eric, for eating my food and never complaining. Thank you for your love and commitment to our family.

Thank you to my amazing mother-in-law, Bonnie, who taught me to entertain with comfort, and that there is no such thing as serving too much food. I miss you.

Thank you to my three perfect babies, Adam, Brian and Rebecca, whose laughter and tears constantly remind me about my priorities in life. By mothering you, I have learned that I can single-handedly (*and one-armed, at that*) run a restaurant to suit all your tastes in the same meal.

It has been an incomparable pleasure to share this process with my dearest friend. Thank you, Cynthia, for your incredible vision for this book. Mostly, thank you for believing in me.

To all new mothers: Everything about a new family takes time. I hope that our book helps you to spend more time with your baby and less time in the kitchen.

Catherine Fliegel

Contents

Introduction

From Cynthia

There I sat in the middle of the kitchen floor at 6:00 p.m. still in my bathrobe, sobbing, cradling my 3-week-old son in my arms wondering if he was ever going to stop crying and if I was ever going to take a shower or cook a meal again in his lifetime.

Necessity being the mother of invention, I did learn to cope—and to entertain with grace and style—even before he went to preschool.

This book is to help those who find themselves completely lost at the thought of making it through meal preparation with a baby in tow. We'll show you how to survive in the kitchen and even consider entertaining.

Many popular books provide excellent advice on child rearing, what to feed your baby, and glorious recipes with tips and techniques for beautiful delicious food. Our book is a little different. Ours addresses how difficult it is to prepare dinner when a fussy baby needs to be held, or other demands distract us from the task at hand.

Being a very organized and practical person, I quickly adapted to life in the kitchen with baby, but I was struck that no one was talking about just how hard this phase of parenting really is. I knew that people weren't eating takeout every night, but how can you make dinner with so little time and only one hand free?

After the birth of my second child, I took notice of how hard this job really was. Over many weeks of commiserating at my girlfriend Jinny's kitchen table (*over the best homemade waffles in town*), we coined the phrase *"a one-armed life"*. I vowed to take notes and really remember these times so that when I had two hands free again, I would write a book that would help others survive this awkward period in the kitchen.

At a holiday meal with friends, a mother remarked that her oldest child was three years old and her baby was six months old, and she had never had her family over for any holiday meal. She said she couldn't imagine how she could pull it off. I told her to start with a small brunch for friends and as she gained confidence, she would be ready for even greater challenges. I told her about cooking meals ahead and putting them in the freezer, and she began to see the possibilities. A few months later, she called in desperation needing some freezer storage tips as she had been cooking in preparation for her family's upcoming visit. Three weeks later, I received a call with thanks for helping her enjoy cooking and entertaining again. The seeds for the book were firmly planted.

Six years passed and I finally sat down to sort my recipes and start writing. Catherine joined me on the project to keep me focused and on deadline. As a fine cook, registered nurse, childbirth educator, and an even better mother, she is the perfect partner. Catherine always admired my organized ways, but organization didn't come naturally to her. Still, where I was unwilling to miss a precious minute of sleep for anyone or anything while my baby was napping or sleeping, Catherine would put her baby to bed and then stay up another two or three hours cooking sumptuous meals and amazing desserts to wow her guests. I love my guests, but not enough to sacrifice sleep. I secretly envied Catherine's energy and spontaneity, and knew she was the yin to my yang.

The result of our collaboration is a treasure trove of delicious and easy meals that you can prepare with baby in tow and will be proud to serve to others. Enjoy.

From Catherine

My in-laws always teased that I never put my babies down, that we were permanently attached to each other. I made no apologies, and with each child I held on longer, savoring the intoxicating smell of their warm, fuzzy heads; their soft, sweet breath on my neck as they slept in my arms; and especially the feedings in the quiet and darkness of the night while the rest of the house slept.

The fact is, I cherished those too-brief early months of being central to my baby's world, before I was traded in for more captivating toys, sippy cups and finger foods, and an exciting new world to be explored on hands and knees.

But hold on as I did for as long as I could, there were still responsibilities to fulfill. While the laundry and the vacuuming could wait, a family must eat. So I found my way back into the kitchen, slowly but surely, open-minded and one-armed.

Little did I realize that only a couple of miles away there was another woman like myself, an accomplished cook, diminished to tears with an overwhelming sense of inadequacy, and completely at the mercy of a person just under 2 feet tall. That woman was Cynthia.

Cynthia and I walked parallel paths, gradually reclaiming successes in our culinary lives with babies on our hips, until one day our paths crossed rather serendipitously. We met because of a special friendship our 2-year-old sons began over wooden blocks and Matchbox cars in preschool.

Our second children were born four months apart and we were each enduring round two of the one-armed life, only this time also with a toddler in- tow. In carpool line and around our dining room tables, Cynthia and I fostered a close friendship. Through the years, our families came together for many meals and holidays, generating mutual respect and admiration in the kitchen.

My mother has a talent for preparing a meal and perfectly timing everything to go from stove to table at the same time. As the roast is standing and waiting to be carved, the gravy is thickening, the potatoes are being mashed, and the green beans are steaming. Having grown up with this example, it was impossible for me to believe what Cynthia professed—that food cooked one to three days ahead, let alone frozen for up to three months, could possibly taste as good as food made fresh before serving.

A few years ago, I had to fly out of town for a family emergency with my return scheduled for the afternoon I was to host a holiday dinner for eighteen people. Rather than disappoint my family and friends by canceling, I decided to proceed with the dinner. I knew I had to let go of the *"make-it-fresh"* concept. With Cynthia as my mentor, I rose to the challenge and decided to give this *"do-ahead"* approach a try. Two weeks before my departure, I prepared the entire meal and froze everything from soup and bread to dessert. My family and guests raved about the meal and touted it as my finest ever. Only Cynthia knew that my husband had defrosted everything in the refrigerator overnight and all that was left for me to do upon my return was to reheat.

The fact that food from the freezer could taste freshly made was a fact more redeeming to me than eight hours of uninterrupted sleep. It changed my entertaining life forever.

When Cynthia asked me to join her on the book project, she was, in effect, trusting me to be a second mother to her *"baby"*. Together we have lived with it, loved it, and nurtured it. We've lost sleep over it, worried about it, and felt guilty when we could not give it our full attention. We have been very, very patient. We have been both protective and critical when necessary and celebrated its little steps with great revelry. Ultimately we have helped it to grow into something special—something we want to share with other mothers like us. I hope that you enjoy the fruit of our labor.

From the moment we began working together, our mission was clear. We would provide easily understandable, how-to kitchen survival information for new parents.

We would strive to inspire, entertain, and inform the reader, ultimately to give her a feeling of competence and confidence as she adjusts to her new reality. We would answer the question *"How can I make dinner with a crying baby on my hip, the phone ringing, the next feeding due in 15 minutes, soon to be followed by yet another diaper change, and I still haven't managed to get into the shower?"*

Our first step toward collaboration was combining our culinary resources. We gathered our favorite recipes and began weeding through them. For each recipe, we called for a manageable list of ingredients that would be readily available at a local supermarket (*no extra trip to a specialty store required*). We walked up and down every aisle in our supermarkets, scoping out convenience items we could substitute into our recipes without sacrificing workability or taste. No fancy culinary skills are required for success with these recipes (*no whipping egg whites; no peeling fruit, dicing vegetables, or mincing fresh herbs; no cutting up a raw chicken*).

Then we began testing, and tasting, and testing again, all with an eye on our kitchen timers and one arm behind our backs. We no longer had a babe-in-arms in either of our families, so Catherine's toddler was happy to be of service.

We can honestly say that these recipes can be made quickly and with one arm—while the other is either tied behind your back or holding a baby.

Since we are both accomplished cooks, we had become accustomed to throwing ingredients together without measuring, and turning a pinch of this and just the right amount of that *"to taste"* into something exquisite. But how much salt and pepper is *"to taste"*? For the first time since our rookie days in the kitchen, we were forced to measure every ingredient that went into a recipe in order to put the recipe in this cookbook. Knowing the recipe would be duplicated time and again by many different people in many different kitchens, we had to forgo our carefree ways. It is our goal that you will be able to produce the same delicious results.

Most of the recipes in this book will not fail even if you don't measure precisely. For example, rather than taking the time and effort to measure out the minced garlic exactly (*as we did for testing purposes*), just grab a common teaspoon from the silverware drawer and scoop out a spoonful. Although the measurement of a teaspoon from your flatware set varies widely, you won't be that far off. Just err on the high or low side according to your own taste buds. As you have more experience and gain confidence, you'll be measuring less often and relying on your eye. It's so much easier to pour a swirl of olive oil from a bottle while holding a baby than to measure it out precisely.

Our families became accomplished taste-testers at our regular tasting buffets. Each member of the clan offered his or her criticism and praise with the practiced style of a county fair pie-tasting judge. Our children have tasted foods that they never would have brought near their lips, all for the sake of the book. We adjusted ingredients and seasonings and added and deleted recipes according to their comments. These dinners will be fondly remembered by both of our families.

In the end, more than 100 recipes survived our criteria, both for taste and ease. They are not gourmet, not fancy, not fussy, and not difficult. They are familiar, simple, easy to prepare, and delicious.

So maybe you're like Catherine, who waits until 5 o'clock to plan dinner. Or maybe you're like Cynthia who tends to be obsessive over her weekly menu plan. Most likely, you fall somewhere in between these two extremes and will find yourself using these recipes to help you cook with confidence—and with a baby on your hip.

Kitchen Safety

Ideally, most people meet the challenge of what to cook for dinner with two free arms. But recognize though, that there are times when the baby is fussy, the clock is ticking, and you simply must prepare sustenance for you and your family. That is why we assembled a full array of recipes that can be prepared while holding a baby on your hip.

There will be times, however, when you will feel safer and more comfortable putting the baby down while you are in the kitchen. You can find a comprehensive list of equipment to keep baby safe and entertained and to help you accomplish two-handed tasks in the kitchen in chapter 3.

Please remember always to use your best judgment regarding kitchen safety. Know your own limitations, and trust your comfort level with any task. We would never put our babies at risk in order to prepare a meal. Letting a baby cry for a few minutes in a bouncy seat is far preferable to risking a burn while you're trying to remove a steaming casserole dish from a hot oven.

These are our recommendations:

1. After handling raw chicken, meat, and raw eggs, always wash your hands thoroughly with soap and water. Clean your work surface with an anti-bacterial spray and paper towels.

2. Placing casseroles into and taking them out of a hot oven is more safely and effectively done with the use of two hands.

3. Broiling and grilling are safer two-handed tasks. If you simply must hold your baby, a back pack will keep him as far away from the heat source as possible. Use long-handled tools to turn your food. Your baby's safety is definitely a much higher priority than a perfectly cooked steak.

4. Sautéing on the stovetop usually produces spatters of hot oil or butter. Keep everyone in your family away from this work area. Most recipes call for only two or three minutes of sautéing, then you can welcome your companions back into the fray.

5. Keep sharp and hot items out of baby's way. Be aware that as your baby grows and develops she will want to grab and reach for things. And what goes in her hand, goes in her mouth. When baby is content to sit and watch, take advantage of her wanting to exercise her independence and enjoy yours.

Just as the clock ticks closer to dinnertime, the days will begin to fly by and soon you will have a toddler diligently scribbling a colorful masterpiece at the table, entertaining himself for longer and longer periods of time, while you are preparing a meal.

Your and your baby's needs and stages will change often, but you will have mastered some tried and true kitchen coping skills which will serve you well for many years to come.

Preparation

If you are reading this book while pregnant, GOOD FOR YOU! It seems that you are interested in being *prepared* for this life-changing event. There are so many things to think about, so many things to do, and thankfully, so many dreams to dream.

Motherhood brings with it so many joys and so many changes to your life. You probably read a great deal on the subject of pregnancy and about how to care for this new addition to your family, but you probably haven't thought much about the realistic changes this new addition will bring to your life.

Your pregnancy lasts only nine months, but your new baby will alter your life for years to come. It's time to get practical and prepare for your new life in the kitchen with baby. Even if you've already had your baby, it's still not too late to get started with an easier strategy in the kitchen. If you are giving birth to your second or third child, this book is still for you. There is nothing like a baby to temporarily turn a household upside down, and we can all use a few more helpful hints and more great tasting, easy recipes to add to our repertoire.

Nesting

In these waning weeks of your pregnancy, the urge to "*nest*" is strong and, just as Mother Nature intended, you'll be making things ready for the baby. There is the nursery to set up and decorate, shopping for booties, diapers, and the cutest little outfits you'll ever see. You'll probably purchase more baby equipment than your parents ever dreamed of owning. Your nesting instinct may extend to organizing and cleaning everything, as well. By all means, go with your instinct as long as you have the energy. The last time Cynthia's house was spotlessly clean and sterile was October 24, 1989—the day she left for the hospital to give birth to her first child. Preparing for the arrival of the baby is surely one of the most rewarding tasks—it is physical work with visual results and it helps you to say *"welcome home"* to your little angel.

Some bundles of joy arrive with only a few days' or hours' notice. If your new addition is arriving by adoption, you may have been dreaming of this day for years, but been unable to prepare for exactly when you would become a family. So, whether your precious gift arrives in the classic nine months, or as a result of a phone call from the attorney, preparation and planning are essential. Start with our advice the minute you can and you will begin meeting the challenges of dinnertime with a measure of finesse.

Preparation

Some mothers-to-be forget, however, about planning and preparing for the real-life impact of a new baby—shopping, baby showers, and baby-related catalogs are a great distraction from reality. If you don't have friends with young children who are giving you some real-world tips and advice, you might be caught off guard on what to expect.

Life with baby is truly wonderful, but it is also a huge adjustment and undeniably exhausting.

Needless to say, some of that *"nesting"* energy is best spent on making your life easier in the early weeks of your baby's life. The most difficult time of day for most families (*of any size and age*) is the late afternoon and dinner hours. Many health practitioners have even suggested that many mom-diagnosed cases of colic are actually cranky babies who know it is the end of the day. Dad is coming home soon, and the attention, focus, and mood of the house will change. Cynthia's son cried from 4 P.M. to 8 P.M. daily for four months. She thought she would never have a normal life again.

Do yourself a huge favor and plan on putting home-cooked favorites in the freezer so that any adult on hand will be able to defrost and reheat dinner.

Family Leave

Our mobile and technologically sophisticated lives today give most mothers some choice in whether to work full-time or part-time, to telecommute or to job share. Still others have the luxury or desire to stay at home full-time. Some may have only a six-week leave after the birth and others may have six months. Whichever of these describes your situation, your common bond with the others is that nearly every one of these mothers is deciding about dinner. The recipes presented here are for all of you. It is up to you whether you make them early in the day, when you rush in the door after work, or on the weekend when you cook and freeze for the week ahead.

Wish List

Performance anxiety reigns during the first year after having a baby. Nowhere does it say that we have to be perfect, but we are constantly comparing ourselves to others and falling short of our own unrealistic expectations. Whether you are pregnant and anticipating this monumental change, or you are currently wallowing in new motherhood up to your tired, sagging eyelids, your perception may be that you need help with the baby. But what you really need is a full-time housekeeper and a personal chef!

Certainly most of us cannot afford these luxuries, but there may be friends or family members who volunteer for the job. Never turn down anyone's offer for assistance, and if you can be so bold, be specific about what you need. If someone with whom you feel comfortable is generous enough to offer her help on an overnight basis, be sure to set the expectations for her visit ahead of time. While your helper cannot wait to *"get her hands on that baby,"* she is better suited to get her hands on that pile of laundry and to cook a splendid meal, so you and your baby can take the time you need to find your rhythm. After each of Catherine's second and third children were born, her sister stayed for more than a week to help with the cooking and the housework and to give the other children some undivided attention; her help and support were immeasurable.

For one reason or another, some good-intentioned loved ones might not be able to offer their time or assistance; however, they can be generous with a gift. When Catherine was pregnant with her first baby, her friends at work organized a baby shower. In lieu of too many receiving blankets, bibs, and unisex outfits, one motherhood-experienced friend gave Catherine a visit from her cleaning service. It was a brilliant and practical gift, and what started out as a one-time indulgence for Catherine, soon became a necessity after the birth of her baby.

In addition to registering at your best-stocked baby store, we suggest you give some thought as to what would make this next phase of your life easier. A department store or home store will stock those practical kitchen items you have been coveting. You might even drop hints to your closest girlfriends about how nice it would be to be pampered by an in-home massage, manicure, or pedicure.

Expectations

If this is your first child, you are exploring uncharted territory. An entire lifetime of living with myths, fairy tales, movies, bad novels, and your own family history are all wrapped up into one large piece of baggage called expectations. You may be surprised to discover deep feelings over certain aspects of parenting and motherhood. Cynthia was sure she was going to keep up her career after her baby was born only to wake up the day after delivery and inform her husband that she wasn't going back to work. Catherine had long-term fantasies of being a stay-at-home mom and knew that her dream would come true and it did.

Expectations can be small, too. Perhaps you expect that you will be a far better caretaker than your spouse, or that you know more about baby care. Be sure to include your partner in both the joys and the routine of parenting. If you don't, you are denying him a feeling of responsibility and caretaking, as well as denying your baby that time and experience with the other parent. But the most important reason is that the patterns and habits you establish right from the start will be with you for a long time and are very hard to change later.

Motivated by guilt when she left her career to stay at home with her firstborn, Cynthia took over the kitchen. After several months, she realized that her husband no longer dabbled in the kitchen to create a gourmet meal. He had dazzled her with extraordinary creations while they were dating (*part of the reason she married him!*), but those days were gone. By taking over the kitchen, along with her perception of what a mom should be, she denied him the opportunity to express himself.

Perhaps creating a *"cooking day"* where you both cook together and put a few meals in the freezer would be a great way to share some kitchen duty. Habits are created early; be sure you are starting out on the right foot. Catherine's husband routinely cooks brunch for the family on weekend mornings, allowing Catherine to sleep late and recharge for the week ahead. This was something he could handle, even with an infant, and now that the children are older, they like to pitch in and help, too.

Starting a family makes you feel like you are creating something for the first time. Take advantage of that shift in your thinking by creating new rituals in your life.

Dinnertime as Ritual

Leaving behind a carefree life consisting of late-night dinners and exotic takeout may seem sad, but it is a wonderful opportunity for change and for creating just the kinds of positive habits we are

Chapter One — Preparation

talking about. Everyone from child-psychologists to mythologists preach the benefits of a family dinnertime ritual. The media bombards us with reports that the cause of the breakdown in our society is the lack of a family dinnertime. They may not be so far off.

As you establish your habits and explore new rituals in your life, take time to establish a family dinnertime. You and your partner certainly need the time together to check in with each other on the events of the day, and rituals created early are likely to be around for a long time. Your baby will soon learn to expect the rhythm of the evening to include that quiet table time. Either on your shoulder, in a swing, or in a bouncy seat, your little one will experience the social dynamics of conversation. Cynthia and her husband always dined by candlelight when they were dating. That dinnertime ritual is still with them today as they dine most nights of the week together as a family by candlelight in the formal dining room.

Today's modern bride typically is not a cook. She did not learn to cook from her mother and in our society of takeout and drive-through everything, meal preparation isn't considered a survival skill. But as you will soon discover, cooking is one of the most basic life skills. You can live as a single person and a newlywed on take-out and restaurant food, but you'll soon be recovering from childbirth and, perhaps, nursing your baby as well and will need a stock of healthy meals. More important for some families, takeout is expensive. If you've lived a single or newlywed life on takeout food, you have

Cooking
as Survival

probably had your fair share of cereal for dinner as well. Break into some new habits by cooking yourself healthy meals and before you know it your baby will be old enough to share your healthy habits with you.

Becoming Well Equipped

If you haven't bothered to stock a kitchen with basic equipment, stop by your nearest home center store—there's likely to be one near the baby store where you've been spending so much time and money lately. This list is rather daunting—don't be intimidated. Add to your current stock one or a few pieces at a time and, before long, you'll be well equipped. Better still, add a piece of equipment to your baby shower wish list—a slow cooker will be a lot more useful than a baby wipes warmer!

Utensils and Gadgets

Wooden chopping board
Plastic or glass chopping board
Set of four nesting stainless steel mixing bowls
Set of three nesting glass mixing bowls
One large plastic mixing bowl with pouring spout
Kitchen timer
Oven thermometer
Can opener
Kitchen shears
Strainer/colander
Tongs
Wire whisk
Long-handled slotted spoon
Long-handled wooden spoon
Long-handled stainless steel spoon
Rubber spatula (*for scraping bowls*)
Flat spatula (*for turning pancakes*)
Pastry brush (*for basting*)

Ladle
Glass measuring cup with handle and pouring spout
Plastic dry-measure cups
Stainless steel measuring spoons
Pizza-cutting wheel
Under-counter jar opener
Freezer-safe storage containers with lids
Freezer-safe resealable plastic bags
Heavy-duty plastic wrap
Heavy-duty aluminum foil

Paring knife	Knives
8-inch chef's knife	
10-inch slicing knife	
Serrated bread knife	

Saucepans with lids and ovenproof handles — **Stovetop**
    (1-, 2-, and 3-quart)
Nonstick heavy skillets with lids and
    ovenproof handles
    (8-, 10-, or 12-inch sizes)
8-quart stock pot with strainer insert and lid

Be sure that you purchase microwave-safe products. — **Bakeware**
Your equipment will be so much more versatile.

Loaf pan—9 x 5 x 3 inch
Square cake pan—8 inch
Square glass baking dish—8 inch
2 nonstick heavy baking sheets *(flat, no sides)*
2 jelly roll pans
Glass pie plate
Glass casserole dish—9 x 13 inch
Glass or ceramic casserole dishes with lids
    (1- and 2-quart sizes, like Corningware)

Heavy roasting pan with rack
12-cup Bundt pan
Heavy enameled cast-iron casserole
  (*called a Dutch oven*) with lid (*3- to 5-quart size*)
Soufflé dishes (*1- and 2-quart sizes*)
Nonstick broiler pan

Make Life Easier

Stand mixer, or electric hand mixer
Food processor
Blender
Slow cooker
Bread machine
Grill
Grill basket
Long-handled grill tools (*spatula, meat fork*)

Special Extras

Cordless can opener
Large mixing bowl with suction bottom,
  or rubber-coated, non-slip bottom
Large pot with single long handle for boiling pasta

Purchase Plan

It's important to remember that you can always add to your equipment. Just keep one rule in mind: buy the best quality you can afford. It is better to own one great chef's knife than an entire set of knives that won't last. Never buy a complete set of cookware. It is rarely practical to own that many pots and pans of one single type. Buy individual pieces of cookware and bakeware that suit the most common cooking tasks. Cynthia simply could not live without her nonstick sauté pan with a lid. She has owned three—the first two were relatively inexpensive and she finally got smart and bought a top-quality pan. Catherine finally received a set of top-quality kitchen knives after putting it on her wish list for a few years. The knives have made so many common tasks easier, she only wishes she had bought them for herself long ago. For any item that will be heavily used, buy the best. Restaurant supply houses are a great resource for top-quality equipment that lasts, although many department and discount stores now sell professional quality equipment at reasonable prices.

Pantry Preparation

Your kitchen should now be well stocked, so it's on to the task of stocking the pantry. Even the most experienced of hostesses can get a little unnerved by short-notice or drop-in guests. And then there are life's constant curves in the road that can thwart our best intentions. There's nothing like an unexpected visit to the pediatrician or even an unexpected phone call to throw the best plan into a tailspin. Anticipating these curves and a well-stocked pantry can see you through. Just as the kitchen equipment list is daunting, our pantry list is as well. Use this pantry list as a guide for making your own pantry list. Storage may be an issue in your kitchen, so you may want to look at some nontraditional areas around the house to store some extras. At a minimum, keep enough on hand for a few meals and surprise guests and you'll be well on your way to staying ahead of the *"what's-for-dinner"* game.

Pantry Stock

Assorted dried pastas
Assorted grains
    (*brown rice, white rice, couscous, grits, cornmeal*)
Dried lentils
Canned beans
    (*lentils, black beans, white beans, chickpeas*)

Canned/bottled vegetables
  (*roasted red peppers, artichoke hearts, marinated
  artichoke hearts, corn, beets, mushrooms, water
  chestnuts, sundried tomatoes*)
Canned fruits
  (*peaches, pears, pineapple, mandarin oranges,
  cherries, applesauce, pumpkin*)
Canned tomatoes (*diced, stewed, crushed*)
Cans/cartons stock or broth
  (*chicken, beef, and vegetable*)
Marinara and pasta sauces
Salsa
Canned fish (*tuna, salmon, clams*)
Cans/jars olives (*Spanish, black, Kalamata*)
  and capers
Canned/dried soups and ramen noodles
Cooking spray
Oils (*olive, canola, vegetable, sesame*)
Vinegar (*distilled white, white/red wine, balsamic*)
Bottled salad dressings
Bottled marinades
Condiments
  (*soy sauce or tamari, Worcestershire sauce,
  ketchup, chili sauce, barbecue sauce, mustards,
  jellies, jams, preserves, chutneys*)
Peanut butter
Assorted breads, crackers, pita/bagel chips, potato
  chips, tortilla chips, breadsticks
Assorted nuts
  (*peanuts, pecans, almonds, walnuts, macadamia
  nuts, pistachio nuts, pine nuts, sunflower seeds,
  salted mixed nuts*)
Dried fruits (*raisins, prunes, mixed diced fruits*)
Canned milk
  (*evaporated milk, sweetened condensed milk*)

Honey
Baking supplies
   (*all-purpose flour, bread flour, sugar, brown sugar,
   cocoa powder, chocolate chips, shredded coconut,
   vanilla extract, cake mixes, salt, baking soda,
   baking powder*)
Dried herbs and spices

Butter and margarine
Cheeses
   (*assorted shredded, grated, cubed cheeses; Parmesan
   cheese*)
Salad mixes (*bagged salads, slaw, fresh baby spinach*)
Precut or ready-to-eat vegetables (*baby carrots,
   cherry/grape tomatoes, celery sticks, broccoli and
   cauliflower florets, baking potatoes*)
Precut or ready-to-eat fruits (*grapes, plums, apples,
   berries, precut melon, pineapple, citrus*)
Eggs and cartons of egg substitute
Prepared pesto sauce, hummus, guacamole, and dips
Refrigerated biscuit and pizza dough and pie crusts
Flour tortillas
Meats (*precooked chicken, ham steaks, cold cuts*)
Tofu
Bottled minced garlic
Lemon juice and lime juice
Sour cream, yogurt, cream cheese, mayonnaise,
   and salad dressing
Cooking wines
   (*dry white/red wines, sherry, vermouth, Madeira*)
Bread machine yeast
Fresh herbs

Freezer	Frozen chopped onions
	Frozen vegetables
	(*spinach, green beans, broccoli, squash, peas, bell peppers*)
	Frozen fruits (*peaches, berries, cherries*)
	Frozen pasta (*tortellini, ravioli*)
	Pie crusts
	Flour tortillas
	Frozen meatballs, chicken tenders, peeled and deveined shrimp

Almost any meal can be made from the pantry and no one will suffer any ill effects from lacking something *"fresh"*. By all means supplement with fresh fruits and vegetables as a usual course of preparation, but if you are stuck one-handed and can't get to the store, your pantry will see you through just fine.

Freezing Means Basic Survival

Once you are well equipped and well stocked, the real preparation begins. As a general rule, Cynthia cooks dinner three nights a week. Two of those meals are made in double quantity so that she now has two cooked frozen meals in the bank. That leaves her with one night for a takeout or restaurant meal and another for an invitation to friends or, failing that, something easy like soup and sandwiches or omelets.

Freezing cooked meals ahead requires just a little know-how. You have several options: plastic freezer bags, plastic freezer containers, and heavy-duty aluminum foil. Whichever method you use, always label and date your container. Use a permanent marker or a ballpoint pen. Some other types of inks

Chapter One — Preparation

may smudge or rub off if they get wet. We promise
you that you will forget what is in the container.
It is very difficult to recognize frozen meals by
sight—they all tend to look dark. Besides, properly
labeled meals make it easier for someone else
to remove and reheat what you want to serve
for dinner.

Buy top-quality resealable plastic freezer bags in
a variety of sizes. Before you add the food, mark the
outside of the bag with the name, quantity, and the
last date you'll consider it fresh enough to eat.
A general rule of thumb for cooked meals is
a maximum of three months. Once you add the
food, remove all of the excess air from the bag. It
isn't the freezer that kills the food—it's the air the
food is exposed to that gives it that *"freezer"* taste.

You can also use plastic containers meant for
freezing. Most freezer containers made today are also
safe for reheating the contents in a microwave oven.
Resist the temptation to use old plastic containers
from food items such as cottage cheese, yogurt,
or margarine tubs. They can crack unexpectedly
in the freezer and you won't know it until your soup
has defrosted all over your countertop. They have
low melting temperatures which can cause them
to leach chemicals if used to reheat food in the
microwave. Aluminum foil is also great for freezing
—just be sure to buy only the heavy-duty kind and
don't forget to label the contents!

If your meal is made up of large pieces of meat,
use a resealable plastic bag and just pop the bag in
the freezer. If it is made up of bite-sized pieces and

lots of sauce, you'll want to place the bag on a cookie sheet in the freezer until it's frozen solid. That makes it easy to stack frozen bags of cooked meals. If you place the bag directly into the freezer on the wire shelving racks, the liquid settles down between the wires and you'll have a hard time removing the frozen bag!

Reheating

You may need some education about reheating. The method that seems to work the best for us is to place the frozen meal, still in its bag, into a microwave-safe serving dish. Vent the bag one inch at the top. Defrost at 50% power for 5-minute intervals. If you defrost at full power, the center does not defrost and the edges boil. When the meal is partially defrosted, transfer the food from the bag into the microwave-safe serving dish to finish reheating. Stir the contents of the dish occasionally to heat the contents evenly.

Food safety is important. Most food is considered properly reheated when it reaches 165 degrees.

If you have not used bags specifically labeled as freezer bags, please remove your frozen item from the bag and place into the dish and cover with plastic wrap. Defrost at 50% power for 5-minute intervals, stirring occasionally.

Be sure to check the manufacturer's instructions for your particular microwave. Many of the newer microwave ovens have preprogrammed defrost cycles that could make reheating even easier. Just remember—be sure that what you have taken out of the freezer to defrost does not have any aluminum foil on it when you place it in the microwave.

You can also defrost your frozen meal in the refrigerator overnight, transfer it to an appropriate pan or baking dish, and reheat it on the stovetop or in a conventional oven or microwave. For sauces and soups, run the container under warm water for 2 minutes, then slide the contents into a saucepan to reheat over low heat on your stovetop.

We recommend having a minimum of ten cooked meals in your freezer ready to go—before your due date! Cynthia had 30 meals in her big deep freeze before her second child was born, and she felt like the richest woman in the world.

Most of the recipes in this book freeze well, but here are our favorites for long-term freezing:

Rice and Lentil Casserole
Mediterranean Chicken
Ham and Cheese Casserole
Meatball Minestrone
Vegetarian Chili
Chicken and Artichoke Casserole
Brisket
Grilled Thai Chicken Thighs and Thai Rice
Rice with Dried Fruit and Nuts
Pasta Putanesca (*Sauce*)

Some of these meals make a complete meal on their own, but we wouldn't mind a green salad with any of them. Some fresh bread would also be nice.

If you are lucky enough to have friends who make sincere offers of help, ask for a meal. It will be a load off your mind and will give you yet another stress-free evening. One of the most thoughtful gifts Catherine ever received came from a dear college friend after the birth of Catherine's third child. When the friend arrived for a visit, she brought two lasagnas—one for the table and one for the freezer.

Drop-In Guests

In addition to preparing ahead for evening meals, we also suggest preparing for the drop-in guest who will come to see the baby. You may not anticipate that you and your new arrival will draw a crowd, but it is highly likely. Not only is it a wonderful feeling to have others "*oooo*" and "*aaah*" over your brilliant creation; it will be wonderful to have the company.

Motherhood—especially in the early days and weeks—can be very isolating and sometimes a bit lonely. You won't be going out on the town as much, and you might not see your friends as often as before. You'll also find out soon enough that a good babysitter is hard to find.

So, by all means, show your drop-in guests how delighted you are that they came over by serving them a little something to eat. It won't be long before you'll be looking for invitations to go over to their houses, and you'll be glad to have been so generous.

Our strategy for drop-in guests is to pick up fresh baked goods at the local grocery store when we're pressed for time, but homebaked sweets and treats

Chapter One — Preparation

are so good. If you can, go ahead and put a few baked goods in the freezer now. Any quick bread, such as our **One Pot Banana Bread,** freezes well and makes a nice accompaniment to a morning or afternoon cup of tea or coffee.

Our **Cheesy Artichoke Bites** also freeze well and are a very impressive appetizer to pull from the freezer and pop in the oven for unexpected guests. Hummus dip with crackers or baby carrots are easy to keep on hand and make a good snack for a late afternoon visitor who might drop by for a glass of wine and a look at the future president.

Preparing for a new baby is such an exciting task. Anticipating the big event is one of life's sweetest pleasures. Along with enjoying these sweet moments of desire and dreams, spend a little time preparing your kitchen to be of service to you during your many hours of need.

The Homecoming

2

It is our hope that you were able to start with chapter 1 and that you have a few things in your freezer to see you through while you are getting back on your feet. Aren't you glad you did? As you are able to cook more meals yourself, try to cook with a double meal in mind so that you are constantly replenishing your freezer stock.

Part of the homecoming period might include a celebration. Depending on your religious tradition, you might be entertaining for a bris or baby naming, or a baptism or christening. If at all possible, this is one of those occasions in life that calls for a caterer. It is unrealistic to expect a new mother to pull off brunch for twenty four while she's not sleeping and still has leaky breasts.

Birth Celebrations

If financial reasons keep you from hiring a caterer, then by all means invite your guests to bring something. If you feel you couldn't possibly ask them to bring something, then perhaps you should reexamine inviting them to such an intimate and significant event in the first place. If they are truly close friends, then they'll want to help and wouldn't be offended if you asked.

Most of these occasions call for a brunch menu. Here is one menu perfect for celebrating your important event. Divide the recipes among your friends. If you are lucky, your grocery store will carry all the items to cover your needs.

Preparing Brunch for 24

With one phone call, they can transfer you from the bakery (*to order your bagels and pastries*) to the deli (*to order your fresh fruit platter, cream cheese and smoked salmon*), and to the floral department (*to order your fresh flowers*). With one stop, you can pick up your orders a day or two ahead, or send someone who has offered to help.

Set out the items for the buffet table the day or night before, if you can possibly spare the room. Have your guests bring their covered dish already warm and have your oven preheated to receive their bounty. Turn on the coffeepot and you're all set.

Menu to Serve 24

Blintz Casserole (*fruit-filled version, doubled*)
Light and Fluffy Cheesy Eggs (*doubled*)
Store-bought bagels, cream cheese, smoked salmon
Store-bought pastries
Fresh fruit platter
Coffee (*cream and sugar*) and juice

1 week ahead

If you are insane and must take on this task yourself, here's the preparation timeline:

Phone or e-mail your guests
    (*save your paper fantasies for birth announcements and birthday party invitations*)
Check for table linens and candles
    (*now is the time to set out any heirlooms or gifts you'd like family to see*)

Be sure to arrange for someone to bring a camera and film—you will have your hands full and it will surely be a day to remember. Consider jotting down a note of who you'd like to be photographed holding the baby so you won't miss anyone.

Make your grocery shopping list and shop for
    casserole ingredients, other menu items,
    and paper goods (*or preferably have someone else
    shop for you*)
Make **Blintz Casseroles** and freeze
    (*up to three months ahead*)
Arrange to borrow a large coffee maker
    and/or thermoses

Phone your grocery store or bakery with your bagel and pastry order (*if ordering bagels, ask them to slice the bagels for you*) Order fresh fruit platter, cream cheese, and smoked salmon Order fresh flowers	1 to 5 days ahead

Pick up your bakery, deli, and floral orders
 	
Arrange the buffet —
    cover the table and add coordinating napkins;
    set out the paper goods, hot and cold cups
    (*for coffee and juice*), and plastic cutlery; set out
    serving utensils; place candles in candlesticks
	1 to 2 days ahead

Prepare two casseroles of **Light and Fluffy Cheesy Eggs**, uncooked, and refrigerate Defrost **Blintz Casseroles** in refrigerator overnight	Night before
Place **Light and Fluffy Cheesy Eggs** in a cold oven. Set oven to 350 degrees. (*This is necessary since the dish is coming out cold from the refrigerator and might crack if placed in a hot oven.*)	1 hour ahead
Start coffee Add the **Blintz Casseroles** to the oven for	30 minutes ahead

30 minutes, until heated through; remove from oven and cover with heavy-duty aluminum foil to keep warm until serving

Set out the refrigerated foods, bakery items, and juice on the buffet

(*If oven space is a concern,* bake **Blintz Casseroles** *1-1/2 hours ahead, cover to keep warm, then bake the egg casseroles.*)

Party Time

Let any guest who offers help bring hot dishes to the table

Be the first one in the buffet line
(*you need the nourishment most!*)

Relax (so baby will, too), and enjoy! As in all aspects of cooking and entertaining, just a few minutes spent organizing a plan of attack can keep you out of a jam.

The Honeymoon is Over

3

Now that the news of the birth is *old* news, and the visitors are few and far between, any help that came in the early weeks is long gone. So it's you and the baby—and that awful question of *"what's for dinner?"*

Whether you are returning to the kitchen with a babe-in-arms solo, or with toddlers or children in tow, sometimes it is difficult to accomplish the tasks you were accustomed to doing without children. Distractions abound and whether it is the cordless phone, cell phone, or the baby's cry ringing in your ears, the dinner hour still looms.

Your stash of prepared meals in the freezer coupled with takeout and delivery will sustain you for only so long. Eventually your pantry stocks will dwindle, your fresh fruit and vegetable bins will empty, and your perishables will perish. Just face the fact. Your venture back into the grocery store and the kitchen with baby is inevitable. But with just a little bit of planning, you and your pint-sized companion can successfully meet the challenges of procuring and preparing food for your family.

Venturing Out

Unless your pediatrician has advised you otherwise, you can safely take your baby out in public as soon as you feel confident and physically ready.

Make sure your baby is appropriately dressed for the outdoor weather. You should bring extra covers (*i.e., a hat and a sweater or receiving blanket*) to keep baby warm in the cooler store environment. Just before leaving home, feed and change your baby so that her immediate needs are met. With a full tummy and a dry diaper, she may even sleep through your entire outing. Of course, bring a fully equipped diaper bag and pack a favorite toy and a pacifier or two, just in case.

Shopping Carts

Shopping cart designers have ingeniously constructed built-in baby seats to keep your baby secured during shopping. While these apparatus address the issues of safety and convenience, there remains the concern about germs. These seats should be avoided unless you have your disinfectant spray and antibacterial wipes handy. There is a variety of equipment available for your purchase and personal use, which keeps your germ pool a family affair and can make your shopping trip much smoother.

Safety

Baby equipment is designed with recommendations regarding age, weight, and developmental stage (*Can your infant hold up her head? Can she sit with support? Can she sit unsupported?*). Be sure to follow the manufacturer's recommendations for safe and appropriate use of the equipment. If you acquire second-hand equipment, check the serial number to make certain the item is not one that has been recalled by the manufacturer (*Consumer Products Safety Commission, www.cpsc.gov, 1-800-638-2772*).

Car Seats

Some infant car seats adapt to fit into stroller bases and even into shopping carts. The seats detach from the secured base in your car and have notches on the bottom constructed to fit snugly and safely into the front section of the shopping cart. This makes the transition from car to store easier, so you can let sleeping babies lie. Be sure that the cart is sturdy enough to accommodate the weight of your infant and the seat. Most large carts you find at your market are probably suitable, but smaller carts such as those you find in a drugstore are not safe. Always leave the restraints fastened securely around your baby, and never leave your cart unattended.

Padded Restraints

There are padded shopping cart restraint systems that can be installed in any cart. Velcro closures secure the baby and support him in an upright and centered position. Cart handle covers accompany the system to protect teething babies from germs and sharp edges. Most devices are machine washable.

Baby Slings

If your baby is one who prefers to be held, or if you like the control of holding onto her, there are many options available.

Baby slings support the baby in a reclining or upright position, in front or back or on your hip, looking in or out. They are designed to distribute the baby's weight evenly across your shoulders and back. Catherine's daughter was affectionately referred to as "*Roo*" for a while, because with a sling, Catherine likened herself to a mama kangaroo. In her "*pouch*" the baby slept, nursed, played, and basked in her mother's warmth and scent, while Catherine shopped, cooked, and even cleaned house, enjoying the closeness.

Baby Carriers

Most major manufacturers of baby items make some sort of baby carrier designed for the baby to be inward and outward facing, and with the parent's optimum comfort in mind. There are many brands and styles to suit any budget.

| Backpacks | Backpacks support the baby in an upright position on your back. They generally have a frame that adjusts to the parent's height, and adjustable seats for the passenger. With his son in a backpack, Catherine's husband enjoyed some *"male bonding"* time while grilling the meat for the family meal.

Be prepared that you may have as many perceived failures as you have successes. Your confidence, if lacking in the beginning, will grow as you schedule more outings. The more adverse situations you face, the more you will learn about yourself, your baby, and your infinite capacity for patience, tolerance, and love.

When all else fails, a good sense of humor is your best coping mechanism.

With or
Without Baby?

Cynthia regards her weekly one-hour grocery shopping trip without children as a sacred rite and enjoys her hassle-free shopping time alone. On the contrary, Catherine has always deemed shopping with her children a special outing, most optimally done at snack time when they eat their way through the store, taste-testing all the free samples. She especially likes to go on senior citizen day. Not only are the samples better and more bountiful, there are scores of surrogate grandparents shuffling around who, with the little ones, find themselves mutually entertained. After such an outing, everyone is ready for a nice nap.

Of course, this approach does not work if you are in a hurry, have a miserable child, or generally despise the task of grocery shopping.

If you absolutely cannot fathom the thought of shopping or cannot muster the energy to get the food, why not have the food brought to you? Do some research and check out the availability of home delivery in your area. Depending on your locale, there are a number of options worth looking into. First, check with your local supermarket. You might be able to call-in, fax, or e-mail your order and have it delivered directly to your door. Some Internet companies offer home delivery of groceries, but access to these services is geographically limited. Whether this becomes your standard practice or just an occasional indulgence, it is definitely worth exploring your options so you can exercise them appropriately.

Alternatives

Okay. The pantry is packed...the refrigerator and freezer are full...the baby is crying...and you are exhausted. It's time to cook dinner! Take some deep breaths like they taught you in childbirth class. You can do this.

Back into the Kitchen

Some people refer to the hour between five and six in the evening as *"happy hour."* Undoubtedly, these people are drinking *and* childless. With a new baby, that hour may be, by far, the longest in your day. You and the baby are equally cranky and needy. Your physical energy is draining, and your creative energy is long gone. First things first. Fix yourself a late afternoon pick-me-up snack. Our **Basic Fruit Smoothie** is the perfect reenergizer and will sustain you until dinner is served. It is also helpful to give some forethought to your evening meals, so preparation is simply a matter of task completion versus a creative process.

Different Styles

Cynthia is a planner. She decides her menus for the week ahead and makes her grocery shopping list based on the recipe ingredients. Her shopping list is constructed in an orderly manner according to the floor plan of her supermarket, so she can zoom aisle-by-aisle down her list. The menus for the week are posted on her refrigerator and consulted before the evening meal preparation.

Catherine is the first to admit that she is not that organized. Or she simply cannot decide what she is in the mood to eat a week ahead of time. That is where a well-stocked pantry is her redemption. She keeps on hand her family's most-used staples and restocks them as she uses them. Rarely does this approach present an obstacle to her evening meal preparation.

We recognize that all people are operationally very different. Some are organized planners, while others have found success in waiting till the last minute. You may find yourself somewhere in between, and perhaps with this new baby, in new territory with regard to your operational skills in the kitchen. Regardless, we recommend you consider your dinner options early in the day. Perhaps when you sit down to enjoy a quiet moment while feeding your baby is the optimal time to resolve the dinner issue. Whatever your personal style, we both contend that planning ahead, anywhere from a week to just hours before, is your best strategy.

It is inevitable that while the stove needs your immediate attention, so will your baby. If he absolutely insists on being held, any of the previously listed carriers which position your baby to your side or on your back are safest for him and give you the most flexibility to work. The sling and backpack are your best options; however, they are not flame resistant. Keep them as far away from your heat source as possible. Your baby's safety should be your highest priority.

Fortunately, most babies are content to sit and amuse themselves for brief periods of time. There is a vast selection of equipment on the market for such babies who wish to exercise their independence, or for even the most skilled cook who needs the luxury of two free hands to accomplish tasks in the kitchen.

Before you go out and buy anything, see what you already have on hand that you can use; or perhaps borrow idle equipment from friends.

Car seats or strollers with their restraints secured can do double duty as an infant seat. Keep baby's favorite toys within reach and change them when she becomes bored. A bouncer seat with a toy bar is the purchasable alternative to this option.	Infant Seats
An activity mat placed on the floor, far enough away from your work area but still within eyeshot of you, is a great entertainer. You can create your	Activity Mat

own activity mat with a colorful quilt and an array of toys or a baby gym. Any experienced mother will tell you that wooden spoons and rubber spatulas, plastic bowls, and pots and pans were her baby's favorite toys in the kitchen. You may even be nurturing a world class chef or percussionist by encouraging the use of such kitchen tools.

Pillow

A specifically designed high-backed propping pillow that completely surrounds your baby can support beginning sitters comfortably.

Swing

We have never met a baby who can resist the rhythmic rocking of a swing. Within minutes of constant back and forth motion, our babies' eyelids became too heavy to hold open and their heads too heavy to hold up. Pure magic. Catherine once put the finishing touches on a four-course holiday meal and set the table for eighteen guests while her first baby slept in his swing.

High Chair

While a high chair does not swing or sway, lull or lose your baby to sleep, it is an excellent place to keep your baby safe and amused. Offer her a selection of finger foods and fun toys. You can even pull the high chair close to your work area so she feels a part of the action. Be prepared to play her favorite game of *"fetch,"* as she throws her things off the tray and you retrieve them obediently. Cynthia even managed to successfully distract her son with his favorite dry cereal and a Sesame Street® video while she gave him his first haircut in his high chair.

A mobile baby can be simultaneously contained and entertained in a stationary walker and activity center. There he can bounce, rock, get an aerobic workout, and spin 360 degrees to locate the objects of his desire. Fun.

Stationary Walker

A portable play yard, portable crib, or gated play yard helps you to keep your crawling or ambulatory infant within comfortable limits. You can place a virtual circus of entertainment in and around and above its periphery to keep your baby happy and engaged.

Play Yard

There are a variety of award-winning videotapes and DVDs designed to stimulate and develop different areas of baby's brain, or videotapes featuring your favorite characters, for baby's education and entertainment. It may be worth investing in a combination portable TV/VCR/DVD player to plug in to your kitchen for baby's viewing pleasure. Make certain that it is AC/DC adaptable so that it also plugs into your car for long road trips for the amusement of passengers of all ages.

Video

You might consider hiring a *"mother's helper"* to help you take the stress out of those late afternoon hours. Usually for only a nominal fee, a young teenage girl, perhaps from your neighborhood or place of worship, could come into your home with your supervision and help entertain baby, fold laundry, do dishes, set the table, or even start dinner, depending on her level of maturity. Eventually you may even trust her to watch baby while you take a nap or escape into a hot bath. Ultimately, her familiarity

Mother's Helper

with the baby and comfort in your own home will make her an ideal babysitter when you are ready to venture out.

You!

Never underestimate yourself. For the longest time, you will be your baby's best entertainment.
She loves to look at you and listen to your voice. So, as your hands are whipping up a fabulous meal, try reciting poetry to her from Mother Goose or Emily Dickinson. Serenade her with your rendition of the alphabet song or the latest Top-40 hit. Or dazzle her with your best Julia Child shtick. We guarantee you will have a captive, adoring audience and not one critic in the crowd.

Tag, You're It!

Eventually, your salvation should walk through the door as expected, if traffic was not too heavy. He will bring with him new energy, a fresh face, adult conversation, two free hands, and hopefully the loaf of bread you reminded him to pick up on the way home. Just give him a kiss on the lips and a one-armed hug, then relinquish your sweet, bundled burden to his expert care. We still employ this *"tag team"* approach to parenting from time to time.

While you are still trying to find your groove, and forever after, there will be days when your evening meal preparation really is impossible. Keep a list of your favorite restaurants that deliver next to the phone so dinner is just a one-armed phone call away. Cynthia has pizza delivery places programed into her phone for such culinary emergencies!

Don't forget your stash of frozen meals. They are there for regular use, but are especially appreciated on those rough and tough days when your best intentions in the kitchen may have been thwarted by your sick baby or your own lack of culinary creativity.

In a year or so, you will undoubtedly look back at your amazing accomplishments and wonder, "How did I ever do that?!" And your answer, along with the answers to so many other similar inquiries will be, "Because I am a mother." And you do what it takes to get through.

Table for Three, Please

4

Eventually, you will want to dine somewhere where someone will serve you instead of it always being the other way around! Go early and often is our advice when it comes to dining out with your baby. Here are some practical tips for making it through the restaurant experience successfully with your baby.

Choose Family-Friendly Restaurants

Family-friendly restaurants have built their names and reputations on catering to young children and families. They are visually appealing and equipped to handle a junior crowd with children's menus, high chairs and booster seats, crayons, friendly wait staff, and sometimes even a floorshow. These niceties may not be important considerations for an infant, but you will appreciate them when you have a toddler. As an added bonus, people who patronize these establishments are less likely to look askance at a crying baby if they, themselves, are among the company of children.

However, there are certainly people, even parents, who forget that babies will cry from time to time. If your attempts to soothe your crier at the table are unsuccessful, move to the ladies' room for some in-depth troubleshooting. The problem may be easy to resolve with a change of diaper or a change of scenery. Or maybe baby just decided to spoil your fun for no apparent reason. No one ever told you babies are rational creatures. If he remains inconsolable, be prepared to leave the restaurant. Even if you have already placed your order, ask for a to-go box, and tip your waiter to help you exit quickly. Then reheat and eat your meal at home

Chapter Four — Table for Three, Please **37**

and chalk it up to experience. At least you did not have to cook!

Frankly, the pre-toddler months are when it's easiest to eat out with your baby and a great time to cut your teeth, so to speak. Be sure to order your favorite foods, definitely those that you cannot prepare at home. Always ask for non-smoking seating.

Power in Numbers

Go with friends who also have babies or small children. When our children were infants, we participated in mother-baby classes. More than teaching important skills, like infant stimulation and massage and postpartum exercises, they provide a wonderful support network through which you can gain social confidence. Catherine and her friends would routinely invade a local restaurant for lunch after class. At any given time, there was more than one baby eating, crying, sleeping, and rattling toys; and more than one mom nursing, rocking, bouncing, and walking with a baby. It was always comfortable and terribly empowering.

Even if you do not take part in formal classes, welcome opportunities to dine out with friends who have babies or small children. When you are among friends, you may feel more comfortable and less fearful of failure.

Go Early

You might be able to take advantage of *"early bird"* specials that many restaurants offer, which makes going out more affordable. Even if you choose an old favorite date spot that is not particularly family-friendly, going early ensures you a table,

Chapter Four — Table for Three, Please

quicker service, and more comfortable surroundings. Simply order your food, eat, then leave. That way, you will avoid *"the crowd"* who chooses a fashionably later dining hour and patrons without children who might look with disdain at the mere presence of a pint-sized person, crying or not. Do not be intimidated by such people, but do be respectful of them. Remember, you chose to dine on their turf.

Go Often

Dining out undeniably offers you respite from the drudgery of evening meal preparation. You deserve it. With that chore out of the way, you might even be able to take a rejuvenating snooze with baby before reservations. The more often you go, the more confidence you will gain, as you learn to deal with all kinds of situations.

As your baby grows, she will become accustomed to the restaurant experience and the socialization that goes with it. From a very early age, all our children knew what their *"best restaurant behavior"* should be. Bottom line, it's a treat for everybody.

However, there were stretches of time we did not go to a restaurant because our babies were teething, enduring a growth spurt, colicky, or otherwise generally cranky during the evening hours. Outings under these circumstances are trying for everyone—even experienced parents. But, these times are normal; babies invariably go through phases during which it is unreasonable to expect a good outing. So don't set yourself up for failure; order takeout or hire a babysitter.

Eat Outside	Weather permitting, dine on an outdoor patio or terrace. The atmosphere tends to be marginally more relaxed. Plus fresh air, coupled with the drone of busy street sounds, can lull a baby to sleep or drown out baby noises for fellow diners.
Ask for Booth	A booth boxes your family in to your own private sanctuary. You can place an infant carrier safely on the bench next to you or on the tabletop, next to the wall. That way, baby is always within reach but away from your dining space and where the wait staff might accidentally spill. Always leave the restraints secured so baby won't topple out.
Bring Your Sling	Your baby may sleep through the entire meal cuddled next to you in your lap, and if he wakes, you can breastfeed him less conspicuously. (*Be sure to place your napkin on top of the sling, as you will almost always dribble*). If you do not own a sling, bring whatever carrier you normally use. It may come in handy if you have to take a walk outside between courses.
Seats are Neat	For older infants who can sit unsupported, utilize a high chair or portable table seat. Most family restaurants provide some sort of accommodations for their tiny patrons or welcome the use of your personal equipment. Be sure to follow the manufacturer's recommendations for safe use of all equipment. Pack a reusable vinyl placemat so baby always has a clean surface from which to eat. Also, check your baby catalogs and stores for sanitary, disposable placemats that attach with adhesive strips to high chair trays and tables for easy cleanup.

Chapter Four — Table for Three, Please

Bring a fully stocked diaper bag. Items you should include especially for restaurant excursions are: diapers, wipes, a changing pad, a change of baby clothes, a bib, and resealable plastic bags (*to dispose of dirty diapers and for carrying wet and soiled clothing, cotton diapers, bibs, and your placemat home*). Bring a pacifier, if your baby uses one; it may stave off having to feed him until you are done feeding yourself. A favorite old toy, or intriguing new toy can provide options for entertainment. Be considerate of those around you by choosing *"quiet"* toys for your little one. While that musical teething ring may be her favorite, twenty rounds of *"Twinkle, Twinkle Little Star"* can be a tad annoying to anyone.

Cynthia still keeps a *"restaurant bag"* in the trunk of her car, packed and ready to go with a few age-appropriate diversions for tabletop entertainment while waiting for dinner to be served. After dinner, the bag returns to the trunk so these items will seem new again at the next restaurant excursion.

Diaper Bag

Bring nourishment for your baby. It is a well-known fact among the ranks of experienced mothers that whenever you bring a forkful of food close to your lips, your baby will want to eat, too. Make sure you go prepared for this inevitability.

If you are bottlefeeding, powdered formula and bottled water mix together easily right at the table. You will quickly become adept at holding your baby and propping a bottle on one arm, leaving the other free to nourish yourself. Or you may have a dining partner generous enough to lend a hand.

Feeding Your Baby

Before you know it, baby will be holding her own bottle.

If you are breastfeeding, choose clothing that will ensure your baby easy access. Specifically designed nursing attire is a luxury but not a necessity. A blouse that lifts up versus one that unbuttons in the front probably provides you the most privacy. A strategically placed receiving blanket or *"nursing bib"* covers everything.

If you and your baby have not yet mastered your breastfeeding technique or you are not comfortable breastfeeding in public, bring a bottle of expressed milk or formula, or find a private place in which to nurse. We both remember the times more than fourteen years ago, nursing our first babies in locked bathroom stalls, sitting fully clothed on the open seat of the toilet. Fortunately, many restaurants and malls now have *"lounges"* or even *"nursing rooms"* with big comfortable chairs that make nursing your baby away from home much easier.

Order from Menu

As your baby gets older you will start to introduce other foods into his repertoire. Pack whatever foods and eating utensils your little gourmand will need for his dining experience. You can even order from the menu for baby, but beware that restaurant food may not be the right texture, or may be too rich or highly seasoned for younger palates. Sometimes little ones will be much more adventurous trying a new food in a restaurant, so don't miss your window of opportunity to expand his tastes.

A good friend of ours suggested eating at Asian-inspired restaurants. You can get plain, steamed rice, vegetables, and tofu or chicken for baby while you enjoy your favorite menu selections. She was even considerate enough of the wait staff to ask for an extra tablecloth to place under the high chair to catch stray grains of rice and wayward vegetables. Always remember the unwritten rule: the greater the mess you leave under the table, the higher the gratuity you leave on the table.

When you are ready for the separation, and when you finally find a person with whom you trust leaving your baby, you will want to reclaim some time alone with your partner (*preferably sometime before your baby graduates high school*).

Ready for Romance

Both of us are guilty of waiting far too long after the births of our first children to schedule that first date with our husbands. While dinner conversation centered mostly on the baby, we managed to cover some current events while we lingered over dessert and decaf cappuccino. Admittedly, as much as we missed our babies, it was nice not to have to rush through a meal and to enjoy some really focused time with our partners. Having learned the error of our ways the first time, we both got back into the dating game much sooner after the births of our other children. This is a difficult step; however, it is an important one to make in order to maintain a healthy relationship with your partner and a strong foundation for your family.

Of course, we can almost guarantee that if you decide to top off your evening in the arms of your beloved, your baby will wake up and put a quick stop to it. A baby is so connected with his mother, he instinctively seems to know when someone else is vying for her attention and that coveted skin-to-skin contact.

Your 1ˢᵗ Dinner Party

Even if it's takeout, you simply must have people over. Using your new baby as an excuse for not entertaining works for a while, but not forever. Eventually you will want the adult company, and you may feel the need to reciprocate with friends who were kind enough to bring in meals when you first came home from the hospital. Let us guide you step-by-step through any level of entertaining you think you're ready for.

Nobody Loves Me

What women miss the most after the birth of their first child is their former camaraderie with other women and anyone able to leave the house without a spit-up stain on their shoulder. One way to beat those *"I-have-no-friends"* and *"who-wants-to-talk-to-a-woman-whose-shirt-needs-laundering-after-5-minutes?"* blues is to have people over. Notice that we don't call it *"entertaining"*—that word even strikes fear in the hearts of people without babies.

Visiting

Having people over means opening your home and your heart to people you would love to spend time with. Keep *"visiting"* as your number one goal, and the rest will fall into place. We truly recommend when you are first getting back on your feet to invite people over for brunch – you and the baby are fresh for the day and you both can nap when it's over!

Cynthia frequently stops herself from inviting guests because when she looks around the house, she simply can't imagine having the energy to clean up the house and cook a meal. She finally developed a strategy to overcome this.

Cleanup Strategy

First, invite only your real friends over—those who already know how hectic life is and accept you for who you are and how you live your life.

Second, walk through the house with an empty shopping bag or laundry basket into which you put any stray messes. Third, dash through the guest bathroom with a disposable cleaning wipe, and put out a fresh set of towels. Done.

Keep it Simple

The most important rule to remember about inviting guests is to keep it simple. No one expects a four-course meal on your Grandmother's china.

Begin your entertaining life with baby with a small brunch. Invite one or two couples. Make one hot dish and serve fresh fruit and perhaps a store-bought baked good. Simple. Easy.

With that success under your belt, you'll perhaps begin entertaining for brunch on a regular basis. It truly is the easiest meal for the cook to prepare and serve.

Plan, Plan, Plan

When you feel up to it, and you are ready for evening guests, take the time to make a plan with a time schedule. Decide on your guest list—don't forget to start small. Plan your meal with the main dish being something you can cook at least a week or so ahead and freeze. Spending a little time organizing on paper will save you from making mistakes and retracing your steps. It is very frustrating to be distracted from your cooking or preparation task by a ringing phone or a crying baby. You might even be distracted for an afternoon

Chapter Five — Your First Dinner Party

or longer with a cranky, teething, or sick baby. Whatever the distraction, once you come back to your task, you've forgotten your place and must spend time retracing your steps. If you spend a few minutes writing down your strategy, you'll be able to pick up where you left off.

There are so many delicious recipes to choose from for brunch, so please use this menu as just a guide. Add as many dishes as you like, and adjust the quantity according to how many guests you are serving. In any case, follow a written plan. That way you'll be sure everything that you intended to serve will actually make it to the table!

Don't overdo it with your table settings—paper and plastic are just fine if that's all you think you can handle for cleanup. We always prefer a regular plate, but if it meant that we wouldn't be able to nap with baby and be stuck with kitchen clean-up instead, then forget it—we'll take paper and plastic any day.

Egg Casserole
Store-bought bagels, cream cheese (*1 dozen mixed*)
Cut-up fresh fruit (*about 2 quarts*)
Coffee (*cream and sugar*) and juice

Your "*to do*" list should look something like this for your first brunch:

Phone your guests
Phone the bagel shop or bakery with your order
    (*if ordering bagels, ask them to slice
    the bagels for you*)

Brunch
Preparation

Menu to
Serve 6

1 week ahead

2 to 3 days ahead	Shop for casserole ingredients, other menu items, and paper goods Purchase fresh flowers, if desired Purchase cut-up fresh fruit Pick up your bagel order, freeze the bagels if more than 1 day before serving
1 day ahead	Defrost bagels in the refrigerator Prepare the **Egg Casserole**, uncooked, and refrigerate
That morning	Set the table
1 hour ahead	Place **Egg Casserole** in a cold oven. Set oven to 350 degrees and bake. Start coffee
30 minutes ahead	Guests arrive Serve juice and coffee Place cold items on the table When you are ready to sit down to brunch, serve the **Egg Casserole** hot from the oven.
Enjoy!	Enjoy your guests, have a delicious brunch with very little cleanup, and when baby naps, reward yourself with a nap, too.
Dinner Menu to Serve 6	When you are ready for dinner guests, here is a very easy meal to prepare, freeze ahead, and serve. It has a very uptown taste, with a casual style. **Chicken and Artichoke Casserole** (*double recipe*) Plain white or brown rice Tossed green salad **Peach Cobbler**

Chapter Five — Your First Dinner Party

Grocery shop for nonperishables and casserole ingredients Make and freeze **Chicken and Artichoke Casserole** Check for candles for the table and decide on dinner beverages	1 week to 1 month ahead
Grocery shop for fresh items, including flowers for the table Prepare steamed rice to serve expected number of guests, according to package directions (*1 cup of dry rice makes 3 cups of cooked rice, or 3 servings*) and refrigerate in microwave-safe serving dish	Up to 3 days ahead
Move casserole from freezer to refrigerator to defrost overnight Set the table; place candles in candlesticks	Night before
Prepare tossed salad early in the day, do not dress; cover and refrigerate	Dinner Party Day
Place casserole in a cold oven. Set oven to 350 degrees and bake.	1 hour ahead
Reheat rice in microwave; add a little water to create steam so the rice does not dry out. Ask a guest to dress and toss the salad just before serving while you mix together the cobbler and pop it into the oven—don't forget to set the timer!	10 minutes ahead

Light the candles and sit down to a delicious job well done!

When your oven timer goes off, remove the cobbler from the oven and set aside. Now dessert is ready for you when you are ready for dessert.

If you start small, and invite friends regularly, you will become comfortable with preparing your meal in advance and truly begin to appreciate the relaxed time you can spend with your guests.

Guests, Holidays, and Relatives

6

The holidays are looming somewhere in the future. There's just no escape from the forward march of the calendar. Every family has some degree of stress related to the holidays, and bringing a new little one into the family only adds to the fray. The demands may be greater on you and your partner to now travel for a holiday, but you may be feeling strongly about starting some new family traditions of your own on your own turf. Your relatives may want to travel from afar to be with you and the baby—and expect to stay with you as well. Whatever route you and your partner decide to take, no need to make a commitment that will be forever. Make a plan you can live with, announce it as your decision for *this* year, and proceed. Try to establish your parental autonomy now while you still can. Transitions are hard for everyone, including new parents.

	Traveling Away from Home

If you travel away from home, you will encounter a level of planning, packing, and transport that you never imagined. On their first out-of-town trip with their firstborn, Cynthia and her husband were astounded at the amount of baby equipment they stuffed into the trunk. Unloading at the hotel resembled a circus sideshow act. It didn't take them long to become seasoned travelers and experts on what to leave at home.

Safety First

Become an instant expert; there are many resources, including books and websites, on traveling with babies and children. Do consult them—they have thought of everything! We recommend that you consider your baby's safety first and comfort second.

Going to Grandma's may mean a smoke-filled house, lots of breakables, dangling window blind cords, unfamiliar pets, and non-childproof medications all within reach of a curious grandchild. Discuss your needs with your hosts before your trip so you can plan for your baby's safety. Ask questions and plan appropriately. It is a bit awkward at first, but this will be only the beginning of checking out the environment your child will be in for many years to come. Before you know it, you'll be asking, *"Are their parents going to be home during the party?"*

You may need to take along a travel play yard in order to have a safe, secure place to set the baby down (*you will have to take a shower sometime!*) and have some peace of mind.

A travel play yard is a lightweight, foldable, and very handy piece of equipment. It can be checked as baggage on an airplane and also fits well into a trunk. If one isn't in your budget, do try to borrow one for any out-of-town travel. And just like our advice for eating in restaurants, travel early and often—your babies will become great travelers.

Simplify Your Expectations

If you'll be home for the holiday, remember to keep it simple. Even people without children place incredible pressure on themselves to try to create a postcard-like holiday celebration and end up living with disappointment.

Strip down your expectations to those you can reasonably accomplish. You might still be fighting sleep deprivation. This is not the time to put on

Chapter Six — Guests, Holidays, and Relatives

a Martha Stewart affair. Pick two or three essential elements for your expression of the holiday and go for each of those all the way. Drop everything else. Your baby won't understand what all the fuss is about and will only know that you are stressed and therefore she will be, too. Give your baby the best gift possible—a relaxed Mom.

With all of that in mind, you may have plans that will include overnight guests at your house—holiday, or otherwise. Cynthia's first overnight guests came when her son was 10 days old. She never got out of her bathrobe as she and her son had yet to become a good nursing *"couple"* and he had his days and nights mixed up. The weekend was a disaster in her mind, although her husband rose to the occasion and took great care of the guests. She quickly learned that her front door was not going to be sealed shut against the tide of guests just because they had a new addition to the family and she had better learn some coping strategies for company.

Your First Weekend Guests

We have selected a confidence-building menu for accommodating your first weekend guests. Follow this timeline and you will see how easy it is to get through the weekend. Make plans early—leaving plans until the last minute is stressful and leaves you with little opportunity to enjoy your guests.

Weekend Menu to Serve 4

Friday Night:
  Mediterranean Chicken
  Plain rice
  Tossed green salad
  Store-bought ice cream

As with all recipes you plan to make ahead and freeze, please be sure to wrap them well in heavy-duty, freezer-appropriate materials.

Saturday Breakfast:
  Self-serve cereals, fruit, yogurt
  Cinnamon-Raisin Bread

Saturday Lunch:
  Tortellini and Bean Soup
  Hearty bread

Saturday Dinner:
  Slow Cook Mock Coq au Vin
  Plain rice
  Tossed green salad
  Blender Pecan Pie

Sunday Brunch:
  Overnight Blueberry French Toast
  Cut-up fresh fruit

1 week to
1 month ahead

Grocery shop for nonperishables and ingredients for chicken dish and pie.

Prepare the **Mediterranean Chicken**, which serves 8. Enjoy half of the recipe for dinner that evening; package the other half in a plastic freezer container and freeze for your guests.

Make the **Blender Pecan Pie**, wrap very well, and freeze.

Up to 3 days ahead

Shop for fresh items, including baked goods you might like to have on hand (*a hearty bread for Saturday's lunch*) and the cut-up fresh fruit for Sunday brunch.

We find that keeping a large supply of fresh fruit on

hand for weekend guests helps to supplement any dietary needs they might not have revealed in advance. Some fresh flowers for the table or the guest room would be a nice addition.

Prepare a double batch of steamed rice; divide into two portions (*one for Friday dinner and one for Saturday dinner*), and refrigerate in microwave-safe serving dishes.

Defrost the **Mediterranean Chicken** overnight in the refrigerator.	Thursday night
Make a double portion of tossed salad. Reserve half in an airtight container in the refrigerator for Saturday night's dinner. Leave off the salad dressing until serving time. Set your table early in the day as well. Guests feel welcome when they see that you have made plans ahead for their arrival.	Friday morning
Transfer the the chicken to a baking dish and reheat it in the oven uncovered for 30 minutes at 350 degrees.	1 hour ahead
Reheat the rice in the microwave; add a little water to create steam so the rice does not dry out.	10 minutes ahead

Toss the salad with your favorite dressing.
Sit down and enjoy your guests.

Be sure to have dinner by candlelight—anything can be forgiven or forgotten over candlelight.

Friday night after dinner	Take just a few minutes to set out the non-perishables and dishes for breakfast on the table before you head off for bed tonight. Put the ingredients for the **Cinnamon Raisin Bread** in the bread machine and set the timer for the morning. Announce that breakfast is self-serve, and whoever gets up first, starts the coffee and enjoys the first slice of **Cinnamon Raisin Bread** warm from the bread machine. No sense in climbing out of bed to serve adults their breakfast if you have been up all night serving a baby.
Saturday morning	Thankfully you made breakfast a self-serve affair so that you can have a little recovery from the excitement of the night before. Once you have had your own breakfast, put the ingredients for dinner into the slow cooker, set the pie out to defrost, and forget about dinner for the rest of the day.
1 hour before lunch	The ingredients for the soup served for lunch come together easily in one pot and take just a very few minutes to prepare. You can set the table and heat the bread while the soup cooks.
Saturday Dinner	No hostess should ever bank on guests pitching in —it seems to be a lost art. If, however, someone does offer to help, accept it graciously when they offer and immediately give them something to do. In this case, it would be nice if someone else set the table for dinner.
10 minutes ahead	Reheat the reserved rice in the microwave with a little water to create steam so the rice does not dry out.

Chapter Six — Guests, Holidays, and Relatives

Transfer the **Mock Coq au Vin** from the slow cooker to a serving platter.

Place the Pecan Pie in the oven for 30 minutes at 300 degrees to warm for dessert.

Toss the reserved salad with your favorite dressing and sit down to a casual, but delicious dinner.

Before heading off to bed, put together the ingredients for the **Overnight Blueberry French Toast** and place in the refrigerator.	Saturday night after dinner
The aroma of freshly brewing coffee will set the morning off to a good start. While your guests are packing up, put the French toast in the oven and bake. Add the cut-up fresh fruit and some juice and you are ready for a fond farewell. As your guests head out the door, pat yourself on the back for a fantastic accomplishment!	Sunday morning 1 hour before brunch
Holiday meals are fraught with anxiety. Uncle John likes the way Aunt Mary makes mashed potatoes and turns his nose up at anything less. Cousin Betty prefers a crown roast for her big meal and brother Joe expects a turkey worthy of a Norman Rockwell painting. This is a losing battle.	Holiday Meals

For five years running after the birth of Cynthia's first child, she ordered the precooked meal offered at her local grocery store for Thanksgiving. It was a pleasure not to have an emotional stake in what got served and what didn't get eaten. After those very liberating five years, she reentered the holiday kitchen as a cook—but one with a new perspective.

On the other hand, Catherine never left her holiday kitchen—literally. She would put her baby to bed and stay awake for hours, preparing spectacular meals to the amazement of her guests. It was as if nothing had changed, except for the addition of a baby seat at the table. But, in fact, things had changed. Her holidays became hurried and hassled, and this was not the kind of message Catherine wanted to communicate to her family who was witness to her craziness. It was not until she learned from Cynthia the value of cooking ahead and freezing that she was able to relax and truly enjoy the holidays with her family and guests.

Accept All Offers

As you prepare your holiday menu, by all means accept any offers to bring a dish. It is so much easier for the hostess to prepare the main dish(es) in her home since it is fairly difficult to transport a substantial main course like a roast or a turkey. If you have given a little thought to your menu in advance, you'll be ready to direct the offers and slot them into your meal planning. Remember to consider your oven and refrigerator space. You may want a balance between reheating in the oven and reheating in the microwave. And don't forget to write down who is bringing what—otherwise you might be eating a five-course meal with three of the courses being dessert.

Here is a holiday meal appropriate for a fall or winter holiday. Substitute your family favorites as appropriate.

Curried Squash Soup
Brisket (*doubled*)
Honey Mustard Chicken Thighs (*doubled*)
Asian Noodle Rice Casserole
Crisp Cauliflower and Green Beans
Orange Glazed Carrots (*doubled*)
Challah (Egg Bread) (*two loaves*)
Chocolate Nut Pie
Blueberry Pie

Grocery shop for all ingredients for recipes you plan
   to make ahead
Decide on and shop for beverages
Check for candles and table linens, if using

1 week to
1 month ahead

Make **Curried Squash Soup** and freeze
Make 2 recipes of **Brisket** and freeze
Make 2 recipes of **Honey Mustard
   Chicken Thighs** and freeze
Make **Asian Noodle Rice Casserole** and freeze
Make **Challah** loaves and freeze
Make **Chocolate Nut Pie** and freeze
Make **Blueberry Pie** and freeze

*Prepare a one-dish meal to serve the night before
   the holiday and freeze it*

Grocery shop for perishables, including flowers

3 days ahead

Set out serving dishes and label with a *"sticky
   note"*—this helps you remember to serve
   everything you have prepared in advance

2 days ahead

Defrost your *preholiday* dinner overnight in the
refrigerator

1 day ahead	Defrost **Curried Squash Soup** in the refrigerator
	Defrost **Briskets** in the refrigerator
	Defrost **Honey Mustard Chicken Thighs**
	    in the refrigerator
	Defrost the **Asian Noodle Rice Casserole**
	    in the refrigerator
	Make the **Crisp Cauliflower and Green Beans**
	    and refrigerate
	Make the **Orange Glazed Carrots** and refrigerate in
	    a microwave-safe serving dish
	Set the table, or arrange the buffet
	
	*Enjoy your one-dish pre-holiday meal with great
	relish—aren't you glad you planned ahead?*

Holiday Morning	Defrost challah loaves and the pies on the kitchen
	    counter. Keep them covered, but loosen the
	    wrapping you used for freezing

1 hour ahead	Put brisket and chicken in oven (*don't preheat for these recipes*) and bake at 350 degrees Reheat soup on stovetop over low heat

15 minutes ahead	Microwave the **Asian Noodle Rice Casserole**,
	    adding a little water to create steam so the dish
	    does not dry out
	Microwave the carrots
	Reheat **Crisp Cauliflower and Green Beans**
	    in a skillet, sprinkle with sunflower seeds,
	    and transfer to a serving dish
	
	*Holiday entertaining is stressful under the best of
	circumstances. With advance planning and freezing,
	your kitchen time is reduced, fewer last-minute
	decisions appear, and you can actually enjoy yourself
	while showing off your little one.*

Baby's 1ˢᵗ Birthday Celebration

7

Congratulations! You made it! You survived! Now celebrate your first year of parenthood right along with your baby's first year. You both deserve it.

The first birthday sneaks up on you. While you are holding on to your sweet, floppy-necked bundle of joy, staring adoringly back at you with a big toothless grin, it is unthinkable that one day very soon, she is going to jump off your lap and walk away from you.

Sleepless nights and endless days witness countless changes for baby. And all the while, as baby is pushing you to your physical limits, testing your competence, and trying your patience, you are learning new things about yourself and changing in less tangible but equally wonderful ways. At the end of the year you find that you have done better than survived. You have succeeded in this new job of parenthood.

Party Planning

So let's celebrate! There are many books written by party planning experts who present creative ideas and thorough plans for making memorable parties. They have thought of everything. Once you find the right book, all that is left for you to do is to find the time and the energy to execute the plan. Good luck.

We do not claim to be experts in this area, though we have each thrown some really fabulous children's parties. Cynthia and her husband were among the first of their friends to have a baby. Their son's first birthday was celebrated in the fashion in which they were accustomed to entertaining. It was an elegant champagne brunch buffet on fine porcelain and linens for a few of their closest friends and family. Catherine and her husband were among the last of their friends to give birth, and she is embarrassed to admit that she got caught up in some heavy party competition. She threw their son a first birthday bash for ten kids and their parents that would have made even the most proficient domestic goddess gasp. Fortunately, the baby handled all the excitement extremely well. But having sacrificed sleep for social status, the mom was pretty overwhelmed. She definitely learned her lesson.

All the experts agree that the first birthday party should be small and short and simple. The only person you need to impress already thinks you hung the moon and is very easy to please. So take our advice, and make it easy on yourself.

Hopefully you have already celebrated some successes as a hostess during your baby's first year. Maybe there was a brunch, a dinner party, a holiday meal, or a weekend with guests. Apply what you have learned from these experiences to culminate your first year together with confidence.

Have a Plan

Our advice to you for this party is the same as for all the others. Some forethought and a written game plan will keep you organized and on track so you can truly enjoy and participate in the festivities. Even the best made plans can be foiled by those first-year molars making a surprise appearance just in time for the party. You may

Chapter Seven — Baby's 1st Birthday Celebration

even have a few first steps to contend with, and that is an entirely different challenge. But after a year, you have certainly learned to be flexible. You can consult your written plan and employ your motherly wiles to pull off a great party despite any obstacles that present themselves.

First, decide whom you wish to honor with an invitation to this monumental event (*remember to think small*). A few close friends and family members who have significantly shared in your baby's first year of life make for an intimate and meaningful gathering. Their faces and laps are familiar to baby, just in case you must devote two hands to your work. Invitations over the telephone or by e-mail should suffice and save you a trip to the stationary store. Schedule the party with consideration of naptime so baby is fresh and ready to party. Clearly define the start and finish times so your guests will head home before baby is partied out.

Invitations

Your table settings should be planned with baby's safety and your convenience in mind. A linen tablecloth or flannel-backed vinyl tablecloth is preferable to those paper table covers with thematic designs. They are cute but too irresistible for your slobbering, dear 1 year old who still puts everything in his mouth. The same goes for the napkins; they are likely to be eaten along with lunch. Use sturdy paper or plastic plates and cups, and plastic cutlery so cleanup will be a piece of cake. A centerpiece of flowers or Mylar birthday balloons are both decorative and festive. Latex balloons pose a choking hazard for little ones and should not be used.

Party Table

Birthday Meal

In Catherine's family, it is traditional for the birthday child to choose the meal and the cake. This tradition started when she was young, and she has perpetuated it with her own children. As a child, her choices were always homemade pizza and banana cake.

Cynthia's family tradition begins with a boxed chocolate cake mix, frosted and decorated to the nines by her and the children. As her children have grown and matured in their artistic abilities, the decorations have evolved from simple sprinkles shaken on the frosting to very elaborate designs squeezed from decorating icing and gel tubes. Certainly you may have your own family traditions you wish to continue or start anew, so please use our suggestions as a guide.

Main Attraction

The celebratory meal should be one suitable for all your guests, including the knee-high sector. Our **Quick-Fix Pizzas** are a perfect choice for this occasion. You can adjust quantities according to your number of guests. Set out a variety of toppings in individual serving bowls, which can be prepared ahead of time, and let your guests construct their own pizzas. Not only does it make your job as hostess a lot easier, it is just plain fun for everyone (*there's your entertainment*).

Preheat your oven and keep it going, so your guests can pop in their pizzas when they are ready to eat. Have your pizza-cutting wheel handy so the pizzas can be sliced into manageable portions and enjoyed especially by you and other guests while holding a baby on one hip. For the younger crowd, you might consider substituting pita pockets for the Italian bread shells and stuffing them with the toppings to minimize the mess. For babies who have not been given the green light for dairy, soy cheese can be easily substituted. Round out your buffet with a tossed green salad and beverages, including juice for the little ones.

Splurge on Cake

While the buffet can be put together easily with baby in tow, the cake is the one area where we suggest you splurge and use two hands. A variation of the Banana Cake recipe in *The Silver Palate Cookbook* is Catherine's absolute favorite and has become her family tradition. When your baby is napping or enjoying some independent activity, take advantage of your two-handed freedom and whip up this fabulous confection (*or perhaps a favorite homemade creation of your own*). The cake can be made a day ahead, covered, and refrigerated until candle-blowing time.

If your pediatrician has not given the go-ahead for eggs or dairy products, your baby will not be indulging in banana cake. Our variation of Baby's First Cake from *What to Expect the First Year* is a better choice, even though it does not make for the same dramatic pictures with frosting all over his hands and face. Coincidentally, we both made this cake recipe for all of our children on the occasion of their first birthdays.

Another Year Begins

Because it is baby's party, she can cry if she wants to—and she probably will. Chances are when she does, she will accept only you to hold her and comfort her. Your one-armed days might diminish slightly after the first birthday, but they are far from over. Teething, tantrums, and tears will require the comfort of a soft hip and warm arms for a long time to come.

After the last guest has left (*and hopefully left you with a clean party room*), congratulate yourself on a job well done. It has been an exhausting and exhilarating day and year. Reward yourself with a well-deserved nap with the birthday baby. And dream sweet dreams of the future and fulfilling your potential as a parent and a cook with two free hands.

Menu to Serve 8	Here is the preparation timeline for a baby's first birthday celebration: **Quick-Fix Pizzas** (*double recipe*) Tossed green salad Soda or lemonade, juice **Banana Cake** and **Baby's 1st Birthday Cake**
1 to 2 weeks ahead	Your "*to do*" list should look something like this: Phone or e-mail guests to have them save the date Check for table linens, birthday candles (*and matches*) Shop for paper goods Make your grocery shopping list for the party
3 days to 1 week ahead	Grocery shop for items on your list (*bananas need to be ripe for the cake recipe*) Your market should carry flowers and a variety of colorful Mylar balloons

Make the birthday cakes and refrigerate	1 day ahead
Place pizza toppings in individual serving bowls, cover with plastic wrap and refrigerate Arrange the buffet: cover the table and add coordinating napkins; put out the paper goods and plastic cutlery (*you will need extra spoons and forks for the self-serve pizza toppings*); set out the beverages and an ice bucket so you won't forget to fill it Line a large basket with a napkin or bright kitchen towel for the Italian bread shells and pita pockets Assemble the salad, except for the dressing; cover and refrigerate Put the centerpiece on the table (*the balloons will be a nice birthday surprise for baby*) Get out the salad tongs, cookie sheets, and pizza cutting wheels	Morning of party
Remove the cake from the refrigerator; place the birthday candles; set out your cake cutter; put the matches in your pocket Set out the pizza toppings with serving utensils Open the Italian bread shell and pita packages and place in the lined basket Fill the ice bucket Toss the salad with the dressing and set on the buffet Preheat your oven to 350 degrees	15 to 30 minutes ahead

Greet your guests as they arrive. Accept all offers for assistance. Take lots of pictures. And enjoy this special time with your baby.

Appetizers

8

Guests, whether invited or unexpected, automatically summon up the need to feed. No matter what the time of day, the size of the group, or the situation, social gatherings call for food. We were probably conditioned from infancy when our mothers delighted us with conversation and song while we nibbled on nipples and slurped from spoons. We still enjoy something good to nibble and slurp with our friendly interchanges.

Fortunately, this is a category where from the jar and from the bag can be a big help. **There are many good-quality prepared foods available in your local supermarket, so you do not have to make from scratch every time you wish or need to entertain.** Keep a variety of entertaining staples on hand, not only for company but for your new grazing habits as well. For a more complete pantry list, refer to our list in chapter 1.

Your pantry should be a fortress of quick fix and ready-made. Canned and bottled vegetables, beans, sauces, and condiments will keep almost indefinitely. Stock an assortment of crackers and chips for convenient snacking and dipping.

Refrigerated items do not enjoy the long life of dry goods, so watch expiration dates. Ready-cut fresh vegetables are more decorative and less fattening than chips and can be munched without guilt. If your supermarket has a salad bar, you may wish to raid it for more diverse but less economical selections. A variety of cheeses and whole washed fruits or cut-up fruits are always popular fare.

Additionally, prepared hummus, guacamole, and various dips and spreads are widely available. A pretty serving dish, a drizzle of olive oil, and a sprig of fresh herb can disguise that store-bought look and flavor.

Your freezer can extend the life of perishable items like cheese and flour tortillas. Nuts and dried fruits stored in airtight containers will maintain their flavor and freshness much longer than on the shelf.

When special times call for special foods, homemade is definitely the way to go. The improvement in quality and flavor goes without saying. **Here we have compiled a sampling of recipes certain to make a big impression with little effort when company arrives.** If you are serving any of our appetizers as an introduction to your main meal, take special care to vary and balance flavors and ingredients.

All of our appetizers can be made ahead. Some can be frozen in advance, then popped in the oven for drop-in guests. Our dips and spreads have the advantage that they can be kept in the refrigerator for several days. With ample time for preparation, plan on serving two or three of them (*depending on the size of your crowd*) with a variety of your favorite crackers and crudités. Their distinctive colors and bold flavors make a remarkable presentation for both the eye and the palate. **Your guests will have a lot of fun dipping and sampling all the possible combinations.** Round out your appetizer selection with salted nuts, imported olives, or a cheese board with fresh grapes. The benefit of finger foods is that they do not require serving plates or utensils; only napkins are essential.

Entertaining does not have to include an entire meal every time. An assortment of ready-made and homemade appetizers may be your best strategy early on. Just open a bag, uncover a serving dish, fill a glass and soon everyone will be happily hovering around the table, nibbling and slurping and getting in a word or two between mouthfuls.

Cheesy Artichoke Bites

We tried this recipe with cholesterol-free egg substitute and reduced fat cheddar cheese. The texture is slightly different, but it is every bit as delicious.

This dish freezes well for up to 3 months. Make an extra batch for the freezer and pop it in a 350 degree oven for 30 minutes when guests drop by.

SERVINGS: 10
PREPARATION TIME: 15 MINUTES
START TO FINISH TIME: 1 HOUR

2 tablespoons olive oil

1 cup frozen chopped onions

1 teaspoon bottled minced garlic

2 (6-ounce) jars marinated artichoke hearts, drained

4 large eggs or 1 (8-ounce) carton egg substitute

1/2 teaspoon salt

1/3 cup Italian-style bread crumbs

Dash ground black pepper

10 shakes Tabasco

1 (8-ounce) package shredded sharp Cheddar cheese or reduced-fat Cheddar cheese

1. Preheat the oven to 350 degrees.

2. Coat an 8-inch square baking dish or pan with cooking spray and set aside.

3. In a medium skillet over medium-high heat, heat the olive oil. Add the onion and garlic, and cook until tender, about 5 minutes.

4. In a medium mixing bowl, lightly mash artichoke hearts with a fork.

5. To the artichoke hearts, add sautéed onions and garlic, and remaining ingredients, stirring well to mix.

6. Pour into the prepared dish and bake 45 minutes, or until golden brown around the edges.

7. Remove from oven and allow to cool completely in the dish, about 1 hour. Cut into 1-inch squares and watch them disappear!

Chapter Eight — Appetizers

Chickpea and Red Pepper Dip

YIELD: 3 CUPS
PREPARATION TIME: 10 MINUTES
START TO FINISH TIME: 10 MINUTES,
                    PLUS 1 HOUR FOR CHILLING

1 (*16-ounce*) can chickpeas, rinsed and drained

1 (*7-ounce*) jar roasted red peppers, drained

1/2 cup nonfat sour cream

1/2 teaspoon bottled minced garlic

1/4 teaspoon salt

1/8 teaspoon pepper

1. Place all the ingredients in a food processor or blender container and process or blend until smooth, stopping to scrape down the sides.

2. Place dip in a serving bowl, cover with plastic wrap, and chill 1 hour.

This rosy dip is delicious with breadsticks and crudités and is sure to be a hit of the party.

Creative Quesadillas

SERVINGS: 4
PREPARATION TIME: 5 MINUTES
START TO FINISH TIME: 10 MINUTES

4 (*8-inch*) flour tortillas
1 (*8-ounce*) package shredded Cheddar,
    Monterey Jack, or Co-Jack cheese, divided

1. Preheat the oven to 450 degrees.

2. Coat each tortilla generously with cooking spray and place sprayed side down on a large baking sheet.

3. Sprinkle 1/2 cup of cheese evenly over each tortilla.

4. Bake for 5 minutes or until lightly browned. Fold in half and cut each quesadilla into two or three wedges with a pizza wheel.

5. Garnish with your favorite toppings.

Tortilla variations: Substitute corn tortillas or gourmet (*spinach or tomato*) flour tortillas for the traditional flour tortillas.

Filling and topping variations: Anything goes, from traditional to extraordinary, whatever ingredients and combinations you can dream up! Raid your pantry or your refrigerator for delectable leftovers and the deli, dairy, and prepared food sections of your supermarket. Sprinkle the filling over half of the cheese and prepare as directed above. Fold other half of the tortilla over the fillings to seal the deal.

From simply cheese to fully loaded, appetizer to main meal, quesadillas are quick and easy and just plain fun.

We recommend you stock up on tortillas and keep a package or two in the freezer.

Some of our favorites variations are:
Refried beans or black beans
  (*lightly mashed with a fork*)
Sour cream
Salsa, salsa verde
Guacamole
Sliced or chopped olives
Diced pimiento
Sliced jalapeno pepper
Minced green chilies
Any spreadable, shredded, or crumbled cheese
  (*like cream cheese, Swiss, feta, gorgonzola,*
  or goat cheese)
Leftover cooked rice
Cooked vegetables
  (*like spinach, mushrooms,* **Grilled Portobello Mushrooms,**
  broccoli, corn, canned diced tomatoes)
Sliced or diced tofu
Cooked meats, poultry, or seafood
  (*like marinated flank steak, cut-up chicken or turkey,*
  grilled shrimp, or smoked salmon)
Shredded or shaved deli meats
  (*like roast beef, turkey, ham*)
Fresh cilantro sprigs

Our recipe is baked,
rather than fried,
for easy large-scale
preparation.

For a single serving,
it is probably most
convenient to cook
the quesadilla in
a large skillet over
medium-high heat
for 5 minutes,
following the same
assembly instructions.

Curried Carrot Spread

We love to serve this spread along with the **Chickpea and Red Pepper Dip**, the **Spicy Broccoli Spread**, or the **White Bean Dip**, and an assortment of crudités, crackers, and crisp breads.

The brilliant colors and contrasting flavors make a special array of appetizers for any size crowd.

Your guests will have a lot of fun dipping and sampling all the possibilities.

YIELD: 1 CUP
PREPARATION TIME: 10 MINUTES
START TO FINISH TIME: 20 MINUTES

12 fresh baby carrots

1/4 cup frozen chopped onion

1 teaspoon bottled minced garlic

1/2 teaspoon curry powder

1/4 teaspoon ground cumin

2 tablespoons olive oil

1/2 cup cannellini beans or Great Northern beans, rinsed and drained

1/4 teaspoon salt

1. In a small covered saucepan of boiling water over medium-high heat, cook the carrots for 10 minutes or until tender.

2. Meanwhile, in a small skillet over medium heat, cook the onions, garlic, curry powder, and cumin in the olive oil until the onions are tender, about 5 minutes.

3. Transfer the cooked carrots and the onion mixture to a food processor or blender container; add the beans and salt; process or blend until smooth, stopping to scrape down the sides.

4. Transfer spread to a serving bowl. Serve immediately, or cover and chill up to 3 days. Let the chilled spread stand at room temperature for 30 minutes before serving.

Garlic Parmesan Spread

YIELD: 3/4 CUP
PREPARATION TIME: 5 MINUTES
START TO FINISH TIME: 10 TO 15 MINUTES

1 stick butter or margarine, softened

1/3 cup Parmesan cheese

1/4 teaspoon garlic powder

1 teaspoon dried parsley

1. In a medium mixing bowl, combine all the ingredients, stirring well to mix.

2. Spread the soft mixture on your favorite bread, or cover and refrigerate until ready to use.

3. For "GCB's," preheat the broiler and coat a cookie sheet with cooking spray.

4. Slice a loaf of French or Italian bread in half lengthwise and place on the prepared cookie sheet.

5. Spread the garlic Parmesan mixture smoothly and evenly over the cut surfaces of both halves.

6. Place on the middle oven rack and broil for 5 to 10 minutes or until the cheese is melted and the bread is golden brown around the edges. Enjoy the best "GCB's" you've ever had!

Catherine's husband says this spread makes the best "GCB's" (Garlic Cheese Bread) he's ever had, and he considers himself somewhat of an expert.

Pesto-Goat Cheese Dip

YIELD: 3 CUPS
PREPARATION TIME: 10 MINUTES
START TO FINISH TIME: 10 MINUTES,
                    PLUS 4 HOURS FOR CHILLING

You will find many uses for this deliciously creamy dip. Serve with pita chips or bagel chips.

3 (*4-ounce*) logs fresh goat cheese, softened

1 (*8-ounce*) package cream cheese, softened

1/4 cup prepared pesto

2 tablespoons balsamic vinegar

1. Place all the ingredients in a food processor and process until smooth, stopping to scrape down the sides.

2. Place dip in a serving bowl, cover with plastic wrap, and chill 4 hours.

Spicy Broccoli Spread

YIELD: 3/4 CUP
PREPARATION TIME: 10 MINUTES
START TO FINISH TIME: 20 MINUTES

2 cups fresh or 1 (*10-ounce*) package frozen
    broccoli florets

1/2 cup frozen chopped onion

1 teaspoon bottled minced garlic

1/4 teaspoon crushed red pepper

2 tablespoons olive oil

2 tablespoons grated Parmesan cheese

1/4 teaspoon salt

1. In a small covered saucepan of boiling water over medium-high heat, cook the broccoli for 10 minutes or until tender.

2. Meanwhile, in a small skillet over medium heat, cook the onion, garlic, and crushed red pepper in the olive oil until the onions are tender, about 5 minutes.

3. Transfer the broccoli, onion mixture, and Parmesan cheese to a food processor or a blender container; process or blend until smooth, stopping to scrape down the sides.

4. Transfer spread to a serving bowl. Serve immediately, or cover and chill up to 3 days. Let chilled spread stand at room temperature for 30 minutes before serving.

A sturdy cracker or pita chip is just the right thing to scoop up this uniquely textured spread. Garlic and crushed red pepper liven up healthful broccoli and bring out the best in our favorite vegetable.

White Bean Dip

YIELD: 1-1/2 CUPS
PREPARATION TIME: 10 MINUTES
START TO FINISH TIME: 10 MINUTES,
                     PLUS 3 HOURS FOR CHILLING

Everyone who tastes this dip wants the recipe! It is one of our favorites and is bound to become one of yours. The ingredients are from pantry staples and pack a high-protein punch. Serve it with pita chips, crisp breads, crackers, or baby carrots.

1/4 cup plain breadcrumbs

2 tablespoons dry white wine or water

1 (*15- to 19-ounce*) can cannellini beans or
    Great Northern beans, rinsed and drained

1/4 cup slivered almonds

1 teaspoon bottled minced garlic

2 tablespoons lemon juice

2 tablespoons olive oil

1/8 teaspoon ground red pepper

1/2 teaspoon dried basil

1/4 teaspoon salt

1. In a small mixing bowl, combine the breadcrumbs and wine or water; set aside.

2. Place remaining ingredients in a food processor or blender container and process or blend until almost smooth.

3. Add the breadcrumb mixture.

4. Process or blend again until smooth, stopping to scrape down the sides.

5. Place in a serving bowl, cover with plastic wrap, and chill 3 hours.

Breads

9

Cynthia frequently asks her husband to pick up a loaf of crusty and hearty whole grain bread on his way home in order to round out a meal. And rarely an evening goes by without bread appearing on Catherine's dinner table. Any type of bread your palate desires is easily acquired these days at your local supermarket or chain bakery. **In spite of this availability, there are times, however, when you need a good smell in the house for a lift in your mood. That's what we think bread machines do best.**

If we were to invest in one piece of kitchen equipment that would give us the most pleasure, it would be a bread machine. To be able to wake up and smell a loaf of bread cooling in anticipation of a morning cup of coffee or tea is one of life's simple and secret pleasures.

After cleaning up the dinner dishes, set up the ingredients for the **Cinnamon-Raisin Bread** and put the machine on *time bake* so that the bread is on it's cooling cycle when you get out of your morning shower. By the time you have put on the coffee or boiled the water for tea, the bread will be ready to remove and slice.

Challah (Egg Bread)

YIELD: 1 LOAF
PREPARATION TIME: 10 MINUTES
START TO FINISH TIME: 3 HOURS, 45 MINUTES

1 cup water

3 egg yolks

1/4 cup vegetable oil

3 cups bread flour

1 teaspoon salt

1/4 cup sugar

1 tablespoon bread machine yeast

1. Add all ingredients into the machine in the order your bread machine suggests.

2. Process on the *basic bread* cycle.

When Cynthia is feeling flush with time, she'll process this recipe for dough, then shape it by hand, let rise until doubled, and bake at 350 degrees for 40 minutes.

Cinnamon Raisin Bread

YIELD: 1 LOAF
PREPARATION TIME: 10 MINUTES
START TO FINISH TIME: 3 HOURS, 40 MINUTES

1-1/4 cups water

2 tablespoons butter or margarine

3-1/4 cups bread flour

1/4 cup sugar

1-1/2 teaspoons salt

1 teaspoon cinnamon

2-1/4 teaspoons bread machine yeast

1 cup raisins

1. Place all the ingredients except the raisins in the bread machine pan in the order your bread machine suggests.

2. Add the raisins when the signal sounds or 5 to 10 minutes before the last kneading cycle ends.

3. Process on the *sweet or basic/white* cycle.

Catherine's brother first made this bread and served it to her for breakfast, warm from the bread machine, lightly glazed on top, and generously buttered. It has never tasted better.

Most bread machine recipes suggest that you add the raisins on signal or before the last kneading cycle ends, but we have placed all the ingredients together in the pan (adding the raisins last) at bedtime, and set the timer for morning.

The distinctive aromas of baking bread and cinnamon awaken the entire house. It's a wonderful way to start the day. We have substituted golden raisins and dried cranberries with fabulous results.

Our favorite topping is butter, of course, but our families enjoy cream cheese and apple butter as well.

Cottage Dill and Onion Bread

Catherine's grandmother and her mother used to make this "dilly" bread by hand and bake it in a casserole dish. She was thrilled to find that it worked well in her bread machine.

Be sure to try this bread toasted.

YIELD: 1 LOAF
PREPARATION TIME: 10 MINUTES
START TO FINISH TIME: 3 HOURS, 40 MINUTES

1/4 cup water

1 cup small-curd cottage cheese

2 tablespoons butter or margarine, softened

1 large egg, slightly beaten

2-1/2 cups bread flour

2 tablespoons sugar

1 tablespoon dill seed

1 tablespoon instant minced onion

1 teaspoon salt

1-1/2 teaspoons bread machine yeast

1. Place all the ingredients in the bread machine pan in the order your bread machine suggests.

2. Process on the *basic/white* cycle.

Herb Cheese Bread

YIELD: 1 LOAF
PREPARATION TIME: 10 MINUTES
START TO FINISH TIME: 3 HOURS, 40 MINUTES

1-1/4 cups milk

1/3 cup grated Parmesan cheese

1/3 cup shredded sharp Cheddar cheese

3 cups bread flour

1 tablespoon sugar

1 teaspoon onion salt

1/2 teaspoon dill weed

1/2 teaspoon basil, crushed

1/2 teaspoon rosemary, crushed

1 tablespoon bread machine yeast

1. Place all the ingredients in the bread machine pan in the order your bread machine suggests.

2. Process on the *basic/white* cycle.

This bread is a tasty addition to any menu, but Cynthia likes to add it to a brunch menu when there needs to be a bread to balance out other sweets on the menu.

To crush dried herbs easily, place them together in a small bowl and rub them between your thumb and forefinger.

Brunch

While recovering from pregnancy and childbirth, then adjusting to your new life with baby, it seems impossible to even think of entertaining. But, you must. There are favors to return and, of course, friends you'd like to see.

If you and the baby aren't doing so well in the sleep department, it may seem like you will never have the energy to carry on a conversation with your guests, much less come up with the energy to cook a meal. Cynthia was unable to keep her eyes open after 7 p.m. and therefore made a lousy dinner hostess.

If you have not had the time (*or courage*) to entertain since the baby was born, you simply must conquer your fears and give this a try.

Our recommendation for new moms is simple—entertain over brunch. A brunch can be as casual or as formal as you would like. On the super easy side of things, you can run out for bagels and cream cheese and put on a pot of coffee. On the formal side of things, you can set the table with fine china and really dress things up. **We prefer a happy medium where our guests feel comfortable in casual weekend clothes, the preparations are done ahead of time, and we all have a relaxing time eating and visiting.** By the time the guests have left, everyone is ready for a nice nap.

Several of the brunch recipes are designed to be mixed ahead the night before. This is a great strategy for new moms. After dinner, toss the ingredients together in a bowl, dump them into a casserole dish, cover, and refrigerate. The next morning, most of these will go into a cold oven and bake for an hour. Time the casserole to come out of the oven about 20 or 25 minutes after the expected arrival time of your guests. That way they get a glass of juice and a cup of coffee first, then everyone gets a hot dish right out of the oven. **After a few successful brunches, you'll be ready to tackle dinner guests.**

Anytime Quiche

SERVINGS: 6
PREPARATION TIME: 10 MINUTES
START TO FINISH TIME: 50 MINUTES

1 cup milk

5 large eggs

1 frozen pie crust

1-1/2 cups shredded Cheddar cheese

1. Preheat the oven to 375 degrees.

2. In a medium mixing bowl, beat the eggs with a wire whisk. Add the milk and mix well.

3. In the bottom of the pie crust, sprinkle the cheese.

4. Pour egg mixture over the cheese. Bake for 35 to 40 minutes or until a knife inserted in the center comes out clean.

A quiche can satisfy any time of day. Add any vegetables you have on hand along with the cheese. Leftover spinach is particularly good in this recipe.

We use quiche as a light supper or weekend lunch, especially when we have to clean out the refridgerator.

We often times have just a little cheese left over in a number of small bags in the refrigerator or freezer. Any combination tastes good baked in a quiche.

Basic Fruit Smoothie

Enjoy this thick and fruity drink as a quick "pick-me-up" late morning or late afternoon when your energy is beginning to flag. With some other nutritional additions, it can substitute for a "meal-on-the-go".

We recommend you buy the economy size packages of strawberries and keep a ready stock in your freezer. Overripe bananas can be peeled, broken into chunks, and frozen in individual recipe-ready freezer bags. The addition of frozen bananas makes the smoothie even creamier.

SERVINGS: 4
PREPARATION TIME: 5 MINUTES
START TO FINISH TIME: 10 MINUTES

2 cups frozen strawberries

1 medium ripe banana, peeled and broken into chunks

1 cup orange juice

1. Combine all the ingredients in a blender container and mix on medium speed until smooth.

2. Add additional juice, if necessary, until the desired consistency is reached.

Fruit variation: Substitute your favorite fresh or frozen fruits like raspberries, blueberries, blackberries, peaches, cherries, melon, or pineapple.

Juice variation: Substitute your favorite unsweetened juice or juice blend for the orange juice.

High-protein variation: Blend in 1 (*8-ounce*) container of plain, vanilla, or fruited nonfat yogurt, and 1/4 cup wheat germ. For added protein and calcium, add 1 cup of skim milk or nonfat dried milk.

Nondairy protein variation: Substitute tofu (*soy*) yogurt and soy milk (*or your favorite milk alternative*) instead of the dairy.

Totally indulgent variation: Add 1/2 to 1 cup of vanilla, strawberry, or peach ice cream, frozen yogurt, or sorbet.

The possibilities are endless!

Chapter Ten — Brunch

Blintz Casserole

SERVINGS: 12
PREPARATION TIME: 15 MINUTES
START TO FINISH TIME: 1 HOUR

1 stick butter or margarine

12 frozen blintzes

4 large eggs

1 (*16-ounce*) carton sour cream

1/4 cup sugar

1/4 cup orange juice

2 teaspoons vanilla

1/2 teaspoon salt

1. Preheat the oven to 375 degrees.

2. Place the frozen blintzes in the bottom of a
   9 x 13-inch baking dish.

3. In a small glass measuring cup, melt the butter
   or margarine in the microwave oven on high for
   2 minutes. Pour over blintzes.

4. In a medium mixing bowl, stir all remaining
   ingredients together and pour over blintzes.

5. Bake for 45 to 55 minutes until lightly browned and
   a knife inserted in the custard comes out clean.

Catherine likes to use cheese blintzes and tops them with fresh or frozen strawberries, blueberries, raspberries, or gourmet fruit spreads. Fruit blintzes really do not need any additional toppings.

Cheesy Potato Skillet

SERVINGS: 4
PREPARATION TIME: 5 MINUTES
START TO FINISH TIME: 35 MINUTES

This stove top "casserole" rounds out your brunch menu nicely. It keeps warm in the skillet while your oven bakes our other delicious brunch recipes. It doubles easily for a larger crowd.

1 tablespoon butter or margarine

1 cup frozen chopped onions

1 teaspoon bottled minced garlic

1 (28-ounce) package frozen diced potatoes or chunky-style hash-brown potatoes

1/4 cup water

1/2 teaspoon salt

1/4 teaspoon pepper

1 (8-ounce) package shredded Swiss cheese or Cheddar cheese

1. In a large nonstick skillet over medium heat, melt the butter or margarine.

2. Add the onions and garlic and cook until the onions are tender and lightly browned, about 5 minutes, stirring frequently.

3. Add the potatoes, water, salt, and pepper, mixing well. Cover and cook 15 to 20 minutes or until the potatoes are tender, stirring occasionally.

4. Reduce heat to low. Sprinkle with cheese; cover and cook 1 to 2 minutes or until cheese is melted.

Egg Casserole

SERVINGS: 12
PREPARATION TIME: 10 MINUTES
START TO FINISH TIME: 1 HOUR

12 large eggs

1 (*16-ounce*) carton cottage cheese

1 (*16-ounce*) package shredded Cheddar cheese

1/2 stick butter or margarine, melted

1 (*8-ounce*) package fresh sliced mushrooms

1/2 cup all-purpose flour

1 teaspoon baking powder

1 teaspoon salt

1/4 teaspoon pepper

1 (*8-ounce*) can stewed sliced tomatoes, drained well

1. Preheat the oven to 350 degrees.

2. In a large mixing bowl, beat eggs well with a wire whisk. Add all remaining ingredients except for the tomatoes, stirring well to mix.

3. Coat a 9 x 13-inch baking dish with cooking spray. Pour egg mixture into dish. Top dish with the tomato slices.

4. Bake for 50 to 60 minutes, until slightly browned around the edges and firm in the center.

If you are watching your cholesterol and saturated fat intake, you can substitute equivalent portions of cholesterol-free egg product for the eggs and reduced-fat cottage cheese and Cheddar cheese, but do not use nonfat cheeses.

For a variation, eliminate the mushrooms and add 1/2 pound smoked salmon (nova or lox) and 1/2 cup frozen chopped onions. Substitute Monterey Jack cheese for the Cheddar cheese.

Grits with Cream

Your brunch guests will feel like royalty when they taste this rich, delicious dish.

This recipe can easily be multiplied up for a crowd.

SERVINGS: 4
PREPARATION TIME: 5 MINUTES
START TO FINISH TIME: 15 MINUTES

1/2 cup quick-cooking grits

2 cups heavy cream

2 tablespoons butter or margarine

1 teaspoon salt

1/2 cup grated Monterey Jack cheese

1. Follow the package directions for cooking the grits, but substitute the cream for the water. Be sure to stir occasionally so they don't burn.

2. Remove from heat and add butter or margarine and salt. Add cheese, stirring well to mix. Serve immediately. The grits can be reheated in the microwave, if necessary.

Hot Fruit Compote

SERVINGS: 8
PREPARATION TIME: 10 MINUTES
START TO FINISH TIME: 45 MINUTES

1 (*16-ounce*) package frozen mixed fruit

1 (*15-ounce*) can mandarin oranges, in light syrup

1 (*8-ounce*) can pineapple chunks, in syrup

1 banana, sliced (*optional*)

1/4 cup brandy

1 (*8-ounce*) carton sour cream

1 tablespoon sugar

2 tablespoons heavy cream

1/2 cup sliced almonds

1. Preheat the oven to 350 degrees.

2. In a 2-quart casserole dish, mix together the frozen fruit, mandarin oranges, pineapple chunks, and banana. Add brandy, stirring well to mix.

3. Bake for 35 minutes.

4. In a small mixing bowl, combine the sour cream, sugar, and heavy cream, stirring well to mix. Pour over hot fruit, top with almonds, and serve immediately.

You can substitute a reduced-fat sour cream, if you wish, without compromising the taste of the recipe, but do not use nonfat sour cream.

Light and Fluffy Cheesy Eggs

This is Cynthia's most-frequently requested recipe. Adults and children alike clean their plates at brunch time.

Cynthia's daughter, Rachel, made a delicious variation using raisin bread spread with cream cheese as substitutes for the white bread and butter.

SERVINGS: 6
PREPARATION TIME: 15 MINUTES
START TO FINISH TIME: 1 HOUR, 5 MINUTES,
                        PLUS CHILLING OVERNIGHT

6 slices white bread

1/2 stick butter or margarine, melted

2 cups shredded cheese, such as Monterey Jack
   or Cheddar

2 cups milk

8 large eggs

1. Coat a 9 x 13-inch baking dish with cooking spray.

2. Arrange the slices of bread in a single layer in the bottom of the dish.

3. In a glass measuring cup, melt the butter or margarine in the microwave oven for 40 seconds on high. Drizzle over the bread.

4. Sprinkle the cheese evenly over the bread.

5. In a large mixing bowl, combine the milk and the eggs, mixing well. Pour over the cheese.

6. Cover with plastic wrap and refrigerate at least 8 hours or overnight.

7. When ready to bake, uncover and place in a cold oven. Then set to 350 degrees. This is necessary since the dish is coming out cold from the refrigerator and might crack if placed in a preheated oven.

8. Bake for 50 minutes. The casserole will be puffy and lightly browned.

Chapter Ten — Brunch

One Pot Banana Bread

YIELD: 1 LOAF
PREPARATION TIME: 15 MINUTES
START TO FINISH TIME: 1 HOUR

1 cup sugar

1/2 cup vegetable oil

2 large eggs

3 large bananas, very ripe

2 cups all-purpose flour

1 teaspoon baking soda

1 teaspoon salt

1 cup chopped nuts

1 teaspoon vanilla extract

1. Preheat the oven to 375 degrees.

2. Coat a 9 x 5 x 3-inch loaf pan with cooking spray and set aside.

2. In a large bowl, add all of the ingredients one at a time, mixing well after each addition with a wire whisk. Pour mixture into the prepared loaf pan.

4. Bake for 45 to 50 minutes. Let cool slightly, and then turn the loaf out onto a platter or board.

Banana bread is another comfort food in our homes. We love it for after school snacks, a late morning cup of tea, and it always appears on our brunch table.

If the bananas are very ripe, just a nice wire whisk will be sufficient to break up the bananas and mix the batter.

Overnight Blueberry French Toast

Catherine loves to surprise her weekend guests with this rich and delicious dish. Pre-sliced loaves of French bread are available on the packaged bread aisle in your supermarket.

If you cannot buy French bread pre-sliced, this recipe is well worth the two-handed effort of slicing it yourself. Simply cut 1-inch slices from a large loaf. Serve individual portions with warm syrup.

SERVINGS: 6
PREPARATION TIME: 10 MINUTES
START TO FINISH TIME: 40 MINUTES

1 large sliced French bread loaf

6 large eggs

2 cups milk

1/2 teaspoon dried nutmeg

1 teaspoon vanilla

1 cup brown sugar, divided

1/2 stick butter or margarine

1 cup chopped pecans

2 cups fresh or frozen blueberries

1. Coat a 9 x 13-inch baking dish with cooking spray. Arrange the bread slices in one layer in the baking dish.

2. In a large mixing bowl, add the eggs, milk, nutmeg, vanilla, and 3/4 cup of the brown sugar, stirring well to mix.

3. Pour mixture evenly over the bread. Cover and refrigerate at least 8 hours or overnight.

4. When ready to bake, preheat the oven to 400 degrees.

5. In a small saucepan over medium heat, melt the butter or margarine and the remaining 1/4 cup brown sugar, stirring well.

6. Top the egg mixture with the pecans and blueberries, then drizzle with the melted butter and sugar mixture.

7. Bake for 30 minutes until set and golden brown on top.

Chapter Ten — Brunch

Pecan Biscuit Ring

YIELD: 1 LOAF
PREPARATION TIME: 15 MINUTES
START TO FINISH TIME: 55 MINUTES

1 stick butter or margarine

1 cup chopped pecans

1 cup brown sugar

1/4 cup maple-flavored syrup

2 cans extra-large size refrigerated biscuits

1. Preheat the oven to 350 degrees.

2. Coat a 12-cup Bundt pan with cooking spray.

3. In a small saucepan over medium heat, melt the butter or margarine and stir in the nuts, brown sugar, and syrup, stirring well.

4. Pour 1/4 cup of the syrup mixture evenly around the bottom of the Bundt pan. Add the biscuits, standing them on edge evenly around the pan. Pour remaining syrup mixture over the biscuits.

4. Place the pan on a baking sheet to catch any overflow and bake for 40 minutes.

5. Cool bread for just 3 minutes and invert on a serving platter. Serve warm or at room temperature.

This recipe is reminiscent of the old-fashioned "sticky buns", but without the fuss.

Spinach and Tomato Frittata

Cynthia is often in a quandary over what to serve for lunch—especially on a weekend and especially if there aren't any leftovers hanging around! Her husband started whipping up an omelet for lunch in an act of self-preservation, and this recipe is a slightly uptown version.

SERVINGS: 4
PREPARATION TIME: 5 MINUTES
START TO FINISH TIME: 25 MINUTES

6 large eggs

1/3 cup grated Parmesan cheese

1/2 teaspoon garlic powder

1/2 teaspoon dried basil leaves

1/4 teaspoon salt

1/4 teaspoon pepper

1/8 teaspoon nutmeg

1 (10-ounce) package frozen chopped spinach, thawed

1 (8-ounce) can stewed sliced tomatoes, drained

1. In a small mixing bowl, beat eggs with a wire whisk. Add cheese, garlic powder, basil, salt, pepper, and nutmeg, stirring well to mix.

2. Coat a large nonstick skillet (with sloping sides and a lid) with cooking spray. Heat over medium heat until hot. Add spinach. Cover and cook 3 to 4 minutes, or until most of the water is evaporated.

3. Spread the spinach evenly across the bottom of the skillet and top with the tomato slices.

4. Pour egg mixture over the top. Cover, reduce the heat to low, and cook for 12 to 15 minutes or until eggs are set.

5. To serve, cut into wedges.

Soups

11

Soup is the ultimate comfort food. Rainy days and runny noses automatically start our soup pots simmering. The aroma lifting off a simmering pot and the flavors mingling in our mouths remind us of happy times. For both of us, soup is love. It nurtures while it nourishes.

Catherine's grandmother would stand over a huge kettle for hours, chopping and dicing and stirring fresh vegetables and stew beef to tender perfection for her family. Each delicious spoonful promised that everything would be all right. Cynthia shows her deep affection for her father-in-law by pleasing him with a perfect matzo ball soup. Not only is it his favorite and that of her holiday guests, but comfort food for her children year-round.

Elegant or informal, light or hearty, starter or mainstay, soup is unequivocally the most versatile element of a meal. **Soup can be sipped by candlelight from fine porcelain with a silver spoon or slurped by firelight from a stoneware mug in your pajamas, according to your inspiration.** A chilled soup can refresh and excite the palate in anticipation of a summer meal, hot from the grill. On a cold winter's day, there is no better meal than a hot bowlful.

Most of our soups are substantial enough to be a main course and need only a plate of simply dressed salad greens and a loaf of fresh bread as accompaniments. Others can be served as a light first course, but be sure to match compatible flavors and ingredients with the rest of the meal.

For example, if you are serving our **Curried Squash Soup** as a starter, choose a green vegetable over squash or carrots as a side dish with your main course.

All of our soups are simple. Most can be mixed in minutes and on the table in half an hour or less. Or they can be prepared up to several days ahead, chilled, and reheated before serving. Feel free to improvise with any ingredients you have on hand—an extra vegetable here, a different herb or spice there. You really cannot fail.

We like to make double batches and freeze the leftovers or ration them for lunches for the rest of the week. **An extra pot of homemade soup in the refrigerator or freezer is well worth what little extra time and effort it takes to multiply the recipe.** Keep ingredients as pantry staples so they are readily available whenever a mood mandates soup. Containers of good-quality broth and cans of diced tomatoes, beans, and lentils are essential. Bottled minced garlic and frozen chopped onions are indispensable.

Though most times a pot of soup is premeditated, it is also one of those meals you can pull off spontaneously when you open the cupboard at 5:00 and wonder, *"What's for dinner?"*

Black Bean Soup

SERVINGS: 4
PREPARATION TIME: 5 MINUTES
START TO FINISH TIME: 15 MINUTES

2 (*15-ounce*) cans black beans, rinsed and drained, and divided

1 (*14 1/2-ounce*) can vegetable broth

1 cup chunky salsa

1 teaspoon dried cumin

1/2 cup sour cream

1. In a food processor or blender, combine 1 can of beans, vegetable broth, salsa, and cumin. Process or blend for 1 minute or until smooth.

2. Pour mixture into saucepan and add the other can of beans. Cook over medium heat about 7 or 8 minutes.

3. Serve in individual bowls with one tablespoon of the sour cream on top of each serving.

Stir up this soup for a satisfying high-protein lunch or a delicious starter for a Southwestern-inspired menu.

Broccoli Cheddar Soup

This is a very hearty soup that tastes especially good on a cold day. It is comfort food for both the adults and children in our families.

We love to serve this soup in bread bowls (small, round loaves that have been hollowed out) as a special treat.

SERVINGS: 6
PREPARATION TIME: 5 MINUTES
START TO FINISH TIME: 30 MINUTES

3 tablespoons butter or margarine

1 cup frozen chopped onions

1/4 cup all-purpose flour

1 (*32-ounce*) container chicken broth

1 (*10-ounce*) package frozen chopped broccoli

1 (*8-ounce*) can evaporated milk,
    or 1 cup of light cream

1 teaspoon salt

1/4 teaspoon pepper

1 (*8-ounce*) package shredded sharp Cheddar cheese

1. In a large saucepan over medium-high heat, melt the butter or margarine. Add the onions and cook until tender, about 5 minutes.

2. Add the flour, stirring well to coat the onions.

3. Add the broth; cook and stir for 2 minutes, until thick and smooth.

4. Add the broccoli, reduce the heat to medium, and simmer for 10 minutes, until tender.

5. Add the evaporated milk, salt, and pepper, stirring well to mix. Cook for 2 minutes, until heated through. Remove from the heat and stir in cheese until melted.

Curried Squash Soup

SERVINGS: 10
PREPARATION TIME: 5 MINUTES
START TO FINISH TIME: 45 MINUTES

1/2 stick butter or margarine

2 cups frozen chopped onions

4 teaspoons curry powder

1 teaspoon salt

2 (32-ounce) cartons chicken broth

4 (10-ounce) packages frozen winter squash

1-1/2 cups Granny Smith applesauce, divided

1 cup apple juice

1. In a large pot with a lid, over low heat, melt the butter or margarine. Add the onions, salt, and the curry powder, cover, and cook for 15 minutes, until the onions are tender and fragrant with the curry.

2. Increase the heat to medium-high, add the chicken broth and bring to a boil.

3. Add the squash and 1 cup of the applesauce, stirring frequently until smooth and squash is defrosted and smooth. Reduce heat to low and simmer about 10 minutes.

4. Add apple juice, stirring well to mix. Cook for 2 minutes or until heated through.

5. Serve in individual bowls with a large dollop of applesauce on each serving.

Squash and apples seem made for each other. Their highly compatible flavors enhance each other splendidly in this earthy soup. Curry lends it an exotic flair. Make this recipe in full and freeze any unused portion.

This soup reheats easily and is a great dish to have on hand for a day that just won't go according to plan.

Cooking for a crowd? This soup multiplies up perfectly for serving to a large gathering.

Meatball Minestrone

This thick and hearty one-dish meal really warms you from the inside out. Hot buttered bread only makes it better. As it sits, the pasta will continue to absorb the liquid of the soup, making it thicker.

If there are any leftovers, you may wish to enjoy the thickened results as a stew or reconstitute the soup with additional broth to your desired consistency.

This recipe doubles easily and is a favorite for the freezer.

SERVINGS: 6
PREPARATION TIME: 10 MINUTES
START TO FINISH TIME: 30 MINUTES

1 cup frozen chopped onion

2 teaspoons bottled minced garlic

1 tablespoon olive oil

1 (15- to 19-ounce) can cannellini beans, undrained

1 (32-ounce) container chicken broth

1 (1.4-ounce) package dry vegetable soup mix

1 (16-ounce) package frozen cooked meatballs

2 (14 1/2-ounce) cans Italian-style diced tomatoes

1/2 teaspoon crushed red pepper

1 cup ditalini pasta, uncooked

1 (10-ounce) package fresh washed baby spinach

1. In a large saucepan over medium-high heat, cook the onion and the garlic in the olive oil until the onion is tender, about 5 minutes.

2. Stir in the beans and chicken broth, and bring to a boil.

3. Stir in vegetable soup mix until dissolved. Add meatballs, tomatoes, and crushed red pepper, and return to a boil.

4. Add ditalini and cook, stirring often, for 15 minutes until ditalini are tender.

5. Add the spinach and stir until it is wilted, about 1 minute.

Mushroom Soup

SERVINGS: 4
PREPARATION TIME: 5 MINUTES
START TO FINISH TIME: 30 MINUTES

2 tablespoons butter or margarine

1 (*10-ounce*) package frozen chopped onions

1 (*8-ounce*) package fresh sliced mushrooms

3 (*15-ounce*) cans chicken broth

1 cup cooked rice

1/2 teaspoon salt

1/2 teaspoon pepper

1/2 cup sherry or Madeira, optional

1. In a large saucepan over medium-high heat, melt the butter or margarine. Add the onions and mushrooms and cook until tender, about 5 minutes.

2. Add the chicken broth and bring to a boil.

3. Add the remaining ingredients, stirring well to mix. Reduce the heat to low and simmer for 20 minutes.

This recipe helps you take care of that little bit of leftover rice from last night's dinner. We like the chunky texture of this soup, but if you prefer, you can chop the mushrooms in a food processor before cooking.

Shrimp Soup
with Tomatoes and Feta Cheese

SERVINGS: 4
PREPARATION TIME: 10 MINUTES
START TO FINISH TIME: 40 MINUTES

1 cup frozen chopped onion

1 teaspoon bottled minced garlic

3 tablespoons olive oil

1 cup dry white wine

1 (8-ounce) bottle clam juice

2 (14 1/2-ounce) cans Italian-style diced tomatoes

1 teaspoon salt

1/2 teaspoon pepper

1/4 teaspoon crushed red pepper

1 pound large peeled and deveined shrimp,
    fresh or frozen

1 cup crumbled feta cheese

1. In a large saucepan over medium-high heat, cook the onion and garlic in the olive oil until the onion is tender, about 5 minutes.

2. Add the wine, clam juice, tomatoes, salt, pepper, and crushed red pepper and bring to a boil. Reduce the heat to medium and simmer for 10 minutes, until thickened.

3. Add the shrimp, and cook 3 to 5 minutes, just until the shrimp turn pink.

4. Add the feta and stir until softened.

It's so easy to throw together the ingredients to this elegant soup for an audience of guests who have gathered in the kitchen to peek at what's for dinner.

You can vary the seafood and cheese in equal quantities to suit your taste.

We especially like the duo of lump crab meat and crumbled goat cheese. Add a crusty bread and simply dressed salad greens, and dinner is served!

Spinach, Mushroom, and Tofu Soup

SERVINGS: 8
PREPARATION TIME: 5 MINUTES
START TO FINISH TIME: 20 MINUTES

2 (32-ounce) cartons vegetable broth

1/4 cup soy sauce or tamari

1/4 cup rice vinegar or apple cider vinegar

2 tablespoons toasted sesame oil

2 tablespoons bottled minced garlic

1 teaspoon ginger

1/4 teaspoon pepper

1 (8-ounce) package sliced fresh mushrooms

1 pound extra firm tofu, drained and cut
   into 1/2-inch cubes

1 (10-ounce) package fresh washed baby spinach

1. In a large saucepan over medium-high heat, combine
   the first 7 ingredients; bring to a boil.

2. Add the mushrooms and cook until tender,
   about 5 minutes.

3. Add the tofu and spinach and cook until the tofu
   is heated through and the spinach is wilted,
   about 2 minutes.

This easy and inexpensive soup is a satisfying main course or starter to an Asian-inspired meal.

If Catherine is serving this as the main attraction, she often throws in some cooked Soba noodles or thin egg noodles and a can of diced water chestnuts. Crushed red pepper is also a nice addition to really spice things up.

Tomato and Yogurt Soup

Cynthia made a batch
of this soup one
evening while dinner
was warming and she
was visiting with guests
in the kitchen.
Everyone stood around
the kitchen island
catching up on the
milestones of the little
ones while slurping
a half-serving of soup
in a teacup, nibbling
on crackers,
and sipping wine.
Perfect.

SERVINGS: 2
PREPARATION TIME: 5 MINUTES
START TO FINISH TIME: 15 MINUTES

1 tablespoon butter or margarine

1/2 cup frozen chopped onion

1 (14 1/2-ounce) can diced tomatoes

1/2 cup chicken broth

1 teaspoon honey

1 cup milk

1/4 cup plain yogurt

1/2 teaspoon salt

1/2 teaspoon dried basil

1. In a medium saucepan over medium heat, melt
   the butter or margarine. Add onions and cook for
   2 minutes. Do not brown the onions.

2. Add the tomatoes. Reduce the heat to low and
   simmer for 3 minutes.

3. Add the chicken broth and honey and simmer for
   another 3 minutes.

4. Stir in the remaining ingredients and simmer for
   a final 3 minutes.

Chapter Eleven — Soups

Tomato Corn Soup

SERVINGS: 4
PREPARATION TIME: 5 MINUTES
START TO FINISH TIME: 15 MINUTES

1/2 cup frozen chopped onion

2 tablespoons vegetable oil

1 (10 3/4-ounce) can tomato puree

1 (14 1/2-ounce) can diced tomatoes

1 (16-ounce) can cream-style corn

1 (5-ounce) can evaporated milk

1/2 teaspoon pepper

1 teaspoon dried parsley

1. In a medium saucepan over medium heat, cook onion
   in oil for 2 minutes. Do not brown onions.

2. Add tomato puree, diced tomatoes, and corn,
   stirring well to mix.

3. Add milk, pepper, and parsley, reduce heat to low and
   simmer, stirring constantly, until hot.

Catherine's children enjoy this soup with grilled cheese sandwiches for a quick dinner before baseball practice.

Tortellini and Bean Soup

*For a fitting accompaniment to this soup, try our **Garlic Cheese Bread** (GCB's).*

SERVINGS: 8
PREPARATION TIME: 5 MINUTES
START TO FINISH TIME: 25 MINUTES

2 (*32-ounce*) cartons chicken broth

2 (*14 1/2-ounce*) cans Italian-style diced tomatoes

1 (*16-ounce*) can chickpeas, rinsed and drained

1 tablespoon bottled minced garlic

1 (*9-ounce*) package refrigerated or frozen
   cheese tortellini, uncooked

1 tablespoon dried parsley

2 tablespoons grated Parmesan cheese

1. In a large saucepan over medium-high heat, combine the chicken broth, tomatoes, chickpeas, and garlic and bring to a boil.

2. Stir in the tortellini, reduce heat to low, and simmer for 3 to 4 minutes, until tender.

3. Add the parsley and Parmesan cheese, stirring well to mix.

Main Dishes

Putting dinner on the table every night is a challenge for anyone. There is the hurdle of deciding what to have in the first place, the next hurdle of shopping for the ingredients, and last, but certainly not least, cooking it.

All of these tasks are more difficult, not to mention more time consuming, with the addition of a baby on your hip. **These recipes are designed to put the main course on your table with great ease and little effort.**

We have taken lots of shortcuts with these recipes. We call for frozen instead of fresh vegetables to eliminate the slice and dice form of manual labor. Do buy the best quality frozen and canned products your store carries. For example, we have found a tremendous taste difference in the different brands of diced tomatoes. If your store carries organic foods, you'll be pleased with the boost in flavor that the organic frozen and canned vegetables have to offer.

We use many convenience items and have usually sized the recipes to call for measurements in terms of the package size rather than a measuring cup. For example, we call for an 8-ounce container of sour cream. If all you have is an opened 16-ounce container of sour cream, you'll need to measure out the 8 ounces. But, if you are making your grocery list, put the 8-ounce size down on your list to eliminate the extra step of measuring.

We have included main dishes designed for an intimate dinner for two up to a barbecue for ten.

Make the recipes that serve four to eight and repackage the extras to freeze for another meal. **Cooked entrees in your freezer are the equivalent of money in the bank. You'll never regret saving for a rainy day.**

Feel free to make substitutions as you go along. We frequently see a recipe that we want to make but lack one ingredient. Look for something similar to substitute and you'll undoubtedly create something tasty without an extra trip to the store.

Please don't limit yourself to this chapter when you are considering your main course options. Sometimes when we are not in the mood for a traditional dinner, we choose one made up entirely of appetizers. When Daddy is working late, all of our children enjoy *"breakfast for dinner."* The Brunch chapter includes many fine choices for this break from routine. Most of our soups are substantial enough to be a meal, and there are a variety of meatless meals available in our vegetarian section. There are so many choices to consider, depending on your pantry stock, your energy level, and your mood.

Beef Stir-Fry

SERVINGS: 4
PREPARATION TIME: 10 MINUTES
START TO FINISH TIME: 25 MINUTES

1 *(14 1/2-ounce)* can beef broth

1 tablespoon soy sauce or tamari

1/4 teaspoon garlic powder

3 tablespoons cornstarch

1 teaspoon vegetable oil

1 pound beef strips for stir-fry

2 cups frozen chopped green peppers

1. In a small mixing bowl, combine the broth, soy sauce or tamari, garlic powder, and cornstarch, stirring well to mix, and set aside.

2. In a large skillet over high heat, heat the oil and add the beef strips. Cook until browned on all sides, about 4 to 5 minutes.

3. Add peppers and broth mixture. Cook, stirring frequently, until the sauce boils and thickens.

Thanks to the convenience items in the butcher's case, dinner is only 25 minutes away with this dish—even less time if you already have cooked rice on hand in the refrigerator.

For a variation, reduce the amount of green peppers and add some frozen vegetables.

Serve over cooked rice.

Beef Tenderloin

There is no finer main dish for a celebration, serving a crowd, or serving important guests. Marinate large roasts in a 2 1/2-gallon resealable plastic bag. Marinating is easier since you just reach into the refrigerator and turn the bag every couple of hours. Snip the corner of the bag with scissors over a measuring cup to capture the marinade.

SERVINGS: 8
PREPARATION TIME: 10 MINUTES
START TO FINISH TIME: 40 MINUTES, PLUS TIME FOR
MARINATING

2 cups soy sauce or tamari

2/3 cup dark sesame oil

1/4 cup bottled chopped garlic

1 tablespoon dried ginger

1 (*3 1/2- to 5-pound*) beef tenderloin, trimmed by
the butcher

1. In a 2 1/2-gallon resealable plastic bag, combine all the ingredients except for the beef, shaking well to mix.

2. Add the tenderloin; turn to coat with the marinade. Refrigerate overnight, turning the bag occasionally.

3. When ready to bake, preheat oven to 400 degrees. Snip a corner of the bag with scissors and drain the marinade into a small saucepan; set aside. Place the tenderloin in a large baking pan.

4. Bake the tenderloin for 20 to 30 minutes until it reaches an internal temperature of 140 degrees on a meat thermometer for rare. Remove meat to a serving platter and let it rest for 15 minutes before carving to allow the juices to be reabsorbed by the meat.

5. Bring the marinade to a boil over medium-high heat; reduce the heat to low and simmer for 5 minutes. Serve with the beef.

Brisket

SERVINGS: 4
PREPARATION TIME: 15 MINUTES
START TO FINISH TIME: 3 HOURS

1 tablespoon vegetable oil

1 (*4- to 5-pound*) brisket, not corned beef

1 teaspoon salt

1 teaspoon pepper

2 teaspoons paprika, preferably Hungarian

1 (*10-ounce*) package frozen chopped onions

1 (*28-ounce*) can diced tomatoes

1 cup water

1 cup red wine

1. Preheat the oven to 325 degrees.

2. In a large Dutch oven over high heat, heat the oil and brown the brisket on the first side for 4 minutes. Sprinkle the brisket with half of the salt, pepper, and paprika.

3. Turn the brisket over and sprinkle with the remaining salt, pepper, and paprika. Cook for 4 minutes.

4. Add the remaining ingredients to the pot.

5. Cover, put in the oven, and bake for 2-1/2 hours.

6. When serving, slice the brisket against the grain and pass the sauce.

Hardly a holiday goes by without this brisket appearing on Cynthia's table. It is her son Norman's favorite meal.

Although this brisket is delicious right out of the oven, it's even better made ahead, frozen, and baked again for another hour on the day of serving.

The Hungarian paprika is readily available and is much more flavorful than the typical paprika.

Broiled Flank Steak

Does this marinade look familiar? It is similar to that which we chose for the **Beef Tenderloin.** This blend of flavors really brings out the best in beef, whether it is an expensive cut for special times, or an inexpensive cut for everyday.

Although this recipe requires about 10 minutes of your attention at the oven, it is easy to prepare and very satisfying to eat.

SERVINGS: 2
PREPARATION TIME: 5 MINUTES
START TO FINISH TIME: 10 MINUTES,
　　　　　　　　　　　　PLUS MARINATING TIME

1/2 cup soy sauce or tamari

1 teaspoon dried ginger

1/2 teaspoon pepper

1 teaspoon bottled chopped garlic

1 tablespoon sesame oil

1/4 cup vegetable oil

1 (*1- to 1 1/2-pound*) flank steak

1. In a large resealable plastic bag, combine all the ingredients except for the flank steak, shaking well to mix.

2. Add the flank steak; turn to coat with the marinade. Refrigerate overnight, turning the bag occasionally.

3. When ready to prepare, preheat the broiler. Snip a corner of the bag with scissors and drain the marinade into a small saucepan; set aside.

4. On a foil-lined broiling pan, place the flank steak and broil on the highest oven rack about 4 minutes on each side or to desired doneness, watching carefully for flare-ups.

5. Remove pan from oven and slice steak diagonally across the grain.

6. Bring the marinade to a boil over medium-high heat; reduce the heat to low and simmer for 5 minutes. Serve with the steak.

Holiday Roast with Madeira Sauce

SERVINGS: 6
PREPARATION TIME: 15 MINUTES
START TO FINISH TIME: 4 HOURS

1 (4- to 5-pound) standing rib roast,
  trimmed by the butcher

1 teaspoon salt

1 teaspoon pepper, plus a dash

1/2 cup Madeira wine

1/3 cup tomato sauce

1/3 cup water

1 tablespoon Worcestershire sauce

1 teaspoon beef bouillon granules
  (or 1 beef bouillon cube)

2 tablespoons butter or margarine

1 teaspoon dried tarragon

1. Preheat the oven to 325 degrees.

2. Place the roast, fat side up, on a roasting pan.
   Season the roast with salt and pepper.

3. Bake for approximately 28 to 30 minutes per pound,
   or until a meat thermometer reaches 140 degrees
   for rare, or 160 degrees for well done.

4. Meanwhile, in a small saucepan over medium-high
   heat, combine the Madeira, tomato sauce, water, and
   Worcestershire sauce, stirring well to mix. Bring to
   a boil and cook for 2 minutes, stirring constantly.

5. Remove from heat. Stir in the beef bouillon until
   completely dissolved.

6. Add the butter or margarine, tarragon, and the dash
   of pepper and stir well to mix them into the sauce.

7. Slice the roast and pass the sauce.

Special holiday meals from our childhood are so comforting when we bring them into our new family life.

A standing rib roast appeared on Cynthia's family's Christmas dinner table year in and year out. You'll find special dishes that will become your family tradition, too.

The sauce is a lovely finish to any grilled or roasted beef. It can be made ahead the same day and reheated just before serving.

Sauteed Veal Cutlets
with Goat Cheese, Wild Mushrooms, and Spinach

SERVINGS: 2
PREPARATION TIME: 10 MINUTES
START TO FINISH TIME: 25 MINUTES

Add some candlelight, soft instrumental jazz, and a bottle of fine cabernet and this is a real recipe for romance.

1/4 cup all-purpose flour

1/2 teaspoon salt

1/4 teaspoon pepper

1 pound veal cutlets

1/2 stick butter or margarine, divided

1/2 cup Madeira wine

1/2 (8-ounce) package wild mushrooms, or sliced fresh mushrooms

1 (4-ounce) log goat cheese, cut into 4 pieces

1 (10-ounce) bag fresh washed baby spinach

1. In a large resealable plastic bag, place the flour, salt, and pepper. Shake to mix the seasonings. Add the veal cutlets to the bag, and shake to coat the veal.

2. In a large skillet over medium-high heat, melt 2 tablespoons of the butter or margarine. Add the coated veal and cook for 3 minutes on each side, or to desired doneness. Remove and set aside; cover with aluminum foil to keep warm.

3. Add the Madeira to the pan drippings and cook for 2 minutes.

4. Reduce the heat to low. Add the mushrooms, and cook for 10 minutes, stirring frequently.

5. Add the goat cheese and remaining 2 tablespoons of butter or margarine, mixing well until melted.

6. Place a handful of spinach onto each of two plates, half of the veal cutlets on top of each bed of spinach, and spoon the desired amount of sauce over the top.

Steaks
with White Beans and Spinach

SERVINGS: 4
PREPARATION TIME: 5 MINUTES
START TO FINISH TIME: 15 MINUTES

2 tablespoons vegetable oil, divided

2 (*10-ounce*) beef top loin steaks

1 tablespoon bottled minced garlic

1 (*15-ounce*) can Great Northern beans,
   rinsed and drained

1/2 teaspoon dried Italian seasoning

1/4 teaspoon crushed red pepper

1/2 cup chicken broth

1 (*10-ounce*) package fresh washed baby spinach

1. In a large skillet over medium-high heat, heat
   1 tablespoon of the oil and cook steaks 4 minutes
   on each side or until desired doneness. Remove steaks
   to a platter.

2. Reduce the heat to medium and add the remaining
   oil and garlic; cook for 1 minute.

3. Add the beans, Italian seasoning, and crushed red
   pepper and cook for 1 minute.

4. Add the chicken broth and bring to a boil.
   When bubbling, add the spinach and cook for
   2 minutes until the spinach is wilted.

5. Cut each steak into two portions and place on the
   individual dinner plates. Top with equal portions
   of the bean and spinach mixture and serve.

This recipe is reminiscent of the flavors of Tuscany. It is an impressive main course to serve, and it is quickly prepared at the last minute.

When you have two hands free, substitute 1 teaspoon chopped fresh rosemary for the dried rosemary. It will take the flavors of this dish over the top.

Wine Marinated Rosemary Rib Eyes

These steaks can also be oven-broiled, but nothing brings out the flavor of summer better than grilling.

SERVINGS: 4
PREPARATION TIME: 10 MINUTES
START TO FINISH TIME: 20 MINUTES,
                              PLUS MARINATING TIME

3/4 cup dry red wine

1/4 cup olive oil

1 tablespoon rosemary

2 tablespoons lemon juice

1 tablespoon bottled minced garlic

1/2 teaspoon salt

1/4 teaspoon pepper

1/4 teaspoon crushed red pepper

4 rib eye steaks, cut 1-inch thick

2 tablespoons butter or margarine

1. In a large resealable plastic bag, combine the first 8 ingredients, shaking well to mix.

2. Add the steaks; turn to coat with the marinade. Refrigerate at least 8 hours or overnight, until ready to cook, turning the bag occasionally.

3. When ready to cook, prepare the grill to medium heat. Remove steak from the refrigerator; snip a corner of the bag with scissors and drain the marinade into a small saucepan; set aside.

4. Place the steaks on the prepared grill and cook for 5 minutes on each side (*for medium-rare*), or until desired doneness.

5. Bring the marinade to a boil over medium-high heat; reduce the heat to low and simmer for 5 minutes; stir in the butter or margarine until melted and serve with the steak.

Baked Chicken

SERVINGS: 4
PREPARATION TIME: 10 MINUTES
START TO FINISH TIME: 1 HOUR, 30 MINUTES

1 heaping tablespoon bottled minced garlic

1/4 cup olive oil

1 tablespoon rosemary, crushed

1 teaspoon salt

1 teaspoon pepper

1 (3-pound) whole chicken

1. Preheat oven to 400 degrees.

2. In a small mixing bowl, combine garlic, olive oil, rosemary, salt, and pepper, stirring well to mix.

3. Place chicken in a roasting pan. Brush garlic mixture on chicken.

4. Cover loosely with foil and bake at 400 degrees for 30 minutes, then reduce the heat to 325 degrees and continue baking for another 40 minutes.

Sometimes you just want the house to smell good, and this dish will do just that. Catherine's good friend, Stella, an accomplished physician, working mom, and quick gourmet, inspired this recipe.

The garlic and rosemary flavors penetrate the tender meat, so it tastes as good as it smells.

This chicken will fall off the bone when done, so just grab a pair of tongs to remove chunks of the whole chicken to serve.

Dried herbs can be crushed with an old-fashioned mortar and pestle or coarsely rubbed between your thumb and forefinger. Crushing releases more of the herb's flavor.

Broiled Lemon Chicken

Here's a low-fat, no fuss version of an old favorite. It is definitely not as indulgent as the traditional fried preparation, but just as tasty.

SERVINGS: 4
PREPARATION TIME: 5 MINUTES
START TO FINISH TIME: 20 MINUTES,
PLUS MARINATING TIME

1/4 cup lemon juice

1 tablespoon vegetable oil

1 teaspoon bottled minced garlic

1 teaspoon thyme

1/2 teaspoon dried lemon peel

1/2 teaspoon salt

1/4 teaspoon pepper

4 boneless, skinless chicken breasts

1 tablespoon brown sugar

1 teaspoon lemon extract

1. In a large resealable plastic bag, place the first 7 ingredients, shaking well to mix.

2. Add the chicken; turn to coat with the marinade. Refrigerate overnight, turning the bag occasionally.

3. When ready to cook, preheat the broiler. Snip a corner of the plastic bag with scissors and drain the marinade into a small saucepan; set aside.

4. On a foil-lined broiler pan, place the chicken and broil on top oven rack 6 to 8 minutes on each side until desired doneness. Transfer chicken to a serving plate.

5. Add the brown sugar and lemon extract to the marinade in the saucepan and bring to a boil over medium-high heat; reduce the heat to low and simmer for 5 minutes. Pour sauce over chicken and serve.

Chapter Twelve — Main Dishes

Cacciatore Style Chicken Thighs

SERVINGS: 4 TO 6
PREPARATION TIME: 5 MINUTES
START TO FINISH TIME: 45 MINUTES

1 tablespoon vegetable oil

1 cup frozen chopped onion

1 tablespoon bottled chopped garlic

1 (*1 1/2- to 2-pound*) package chicken thighs, about 8

1/2 cup white wine or chicken broth

1 (*28-ounce*) can diced tomatoes

2 teaspoons dried Italian seasoning

1. In a large deep skillet with a lid, heat the oil over medium-high heat. Add onion and garlic and cook 1 to 2 minutes.

2. Add chicken thighs, skin side down, and brown for 5 to 6 minutes.

3. Turn thighs to other side. Add wine, if using, or chicken broth, then the tomatoes and Italian seasoning.

4. Reduce heat to low, cover, and cook for 35 minutes, stirring occasionally.

The ingredients to this recipe sometimes get changed just a bit when Cynthia prepares this dish from memory, but it always tastes great.

The extra step of browning the chicken thighs gives this recipe a real boost in flavor.- It's worth those five extra minutes at the stove.

Chicken and Artichoke Casserole

This dish is a recipe
served by Cynthia's
dear friend, Anne
Rivers Siddons,
who entertains with
enviable grace and
ease. We took the
liberty of making a few
shortcuts, but with no
loss in flavor.
This recipe easily
doubles to serve 8 for a
dinner party.

SERVINGS: 4
PREPARATION TIME: 10 MINUTES
START TO FINISH TIME: 45 MINUTES

2 teaspoons vegetable oil

1 pound chicken breast tenders

1 teaspoon bottled chopped garlic

1 (10-ounce) package frozen artichoke hearts, defrosted

1 (8-ounce) package fresh sliced mushrooms

1 (12-ounce) can evaporated milk

1 (14 1/2-ounce) can diced tomatoes

1 teaspoon dried basil

1 teaspoon dried tarragon

1/2 teaspoon salt

1/4 cup sherry, optional

1/4 cup sliced almonds

1. Preheat oven to 350 degrees.

2. In a large pan over medium-high heat, heat the oil
   and cook the chicken tenders 3 to 4 minutes to
   brown them slightly.

3. Add the garlic, artichoke hearts, and mushrooms to
   the pan and saute them with the chicken for another
   3 to 4 minutes.

4. In a medium mixing bowl, combine the milk,
   tomatoes, basil, tarragon, salt, and sherry, if using,
   stirring well to mix.

5. Add the chicken, artichoke, and mushroom mixture
   to the milk and tomato mixture, mixing well.

6. Coat a baking dish with cooking spray. Add contents
   of mixing bowl. Top with almonds.

7. Bake 25 to 35 minutes, until sauce is bubbly.

Chapter Twelve — Main Dishes

Grilled Thai Chicken Thighs

SERVINGS: 8
PREPARATION TIME: 10 MINUTES
START TO FINISH TIME: 20 MINUTES,
                            PLUS MARINATING TIME

1/2 cup mango chutney

1/3 cup pineapple juice

1/3 cup soy sauce or tamari

1/2 teaspoon bottled minced garlic

1/4 cup vegetable oil

2 pounds boneless and skinless chicken thighs,
   about 12 to 14 pieces

1. Combine all the ingredients, except the chicken,
   in a blender container and blend until the marinade
   is smooth.

2. Transfer the marinade to a large resealable plastic bag.
   Add chicken thighs; turn to coat with the marinade.
   Refrigerate at least 1 hour or overnight, turning the
   bag occasionally.

3. When ready to cook, prepare the grill to medium
   heat.

4. Place chicken on hot grill and cook 5 minutes on
   each side, or until desired doneness. Discard the
   remaining marinade.

The Thai-style marinade is an intriguing blend of exotic flavors that makes the chicken moist and flavorful.

Depending on your preference, boneless and skinless chicken breasts or peeled and deveined shrimp work equally well in this recipe. Simply adjust the grilling time appropriately for desired doneness.

If you are serving a smaller crowd, by all means make the entire recipe through step 2. Place half of the uncooked portion in a plastic freezer bag and bank it in the freezer for the future. When you are ready to enjoy it again, defrost the marinated chicken in the refrigerator overnight and proceed with steps 3 and 4.

Mediterranean Chicken

This recipe is an adaptation from The Silver Palate's Chicken Marbella. It is Catherine's all-time favorite party dish. We have doubled the recipe for larger groups, but never made less than this recipe calls for. The leftovers are even better! We have made this spectacular dish even fruitier and more manageable for the one-armed cook.

SERVINGS: 8
PREPARATION TIME: 10 MINUTES
START TO FINISH TIME: 1 HOUR, 10 MINUTES,
                    PLUS MARINATING TIME

1 heaping tablespoon bottled minced garlic

1/4 cup oregano

1 teaspoon salt

1/4 teaspoon pepper

1/2 cup red wine vinegar

1/2 cup olive oil

1 (12-ounce) bag bite-size pitted prunes

1 (7-ounce) jar pitted Spanish green olives, drained

1 (3 1/2-ounce) jar capers, drained,

6 dried whole bay leaves

8 pieces chicken breast quarters or chicken thigh/leg quarters, or a mixture of both

1 cup brown sugar

1 cup dry white wine

1. In a 2 1/2-gallon resealable plastic bag, combine the first 10 ingredients, shaking well to mix.

2. Add the chicken pieces; turn to coat with the marinade. Refrigerate overnight, turning the bag occasionally.

3. When ready to cook, preheat the oven to 350 degrees.

4. In one or two large, shallow baking pans, arrange the chicken, skin side up, and pour the marinade evenly over it.

5. In a medium mixing bowl, combine the brown sugar and white wine, mixing well. Pour this mixture evenly over the chicken.

6. Bake for 50 minutes to 1 hour, until the chicken is tender.

7. Change oven setting to broil; broil chicken until skin is crisp and golden brown. Remove from oven.

8. Transfer chicken, prunes, olives, and capers to a serving platter. Moisten with a few spoonfuls of pan juices and pass the remaining juices.

Chicken quarters are available in economy-size family packs.

Plain white or brown rice is the perfect accompaniment to this dish, as it soaks up the delicious pan juices.

My Chicken Thighs

This dish appears repeatedly on Cynthia's holiday menu—there would be mutiny if it didn't.

This recipe doubles or halves easily.

The thighs can be prepared in the marinade and frozen up to 3 months. Defrost in the refrigerator, place in a cold oven, and bake at 350 degrees for about 1-1/2 hours.

SERVINGS: 8
PREPARATION TIME: 10 MINUTES
START TO FINISH TIME: 1 HOUR, 10 MINUTES,
                               PLUS MARINATING TIME

1/2 cup honey-flavored mustard

1/2 cup honey

3/4 cup vegetable oil

2 pounds boneless and skinless chicken thighs, about 12 to 14 pieces

1. In a large resealable plastic bag, combine the first 3 ingredients, shaking well to mix.

2. Add the chicken pieces; turn to coat with the marinade. Refrigerate 8 hours or overnight, turning the bag occasionally.

3. When ready to cook, preheat the oven to 350 degrees.

4. Coat a 9 x 13-inch baking pan with cooking spray. Remove the chicken from the bag with tongs and place skin side up in the pan. Discard the marinade.

5. Bake for 50 minutes to 1 hour, until the chicken is tender.

Variation: For flavors reminiscent of Indian cuisine, add 1 tablespoon curry powder to the marinade and sprinkle the cooked chicken with 1/4 cup grated coconut.

Nearly Instant Stir-Fry

SERVINGS: 4
PREPARATION TIME: 5 MINUTES
START TO FINISH TIME: 12 MINUTES

1 (1-pound) package chicken breast tenders

1/2 cup bottled stir-fry sauce, divided

1 (16-ounce) package fresh-cut broccoli stir-fry mix

1/4 cup water

1. In a medium mixing bowl, place the chicken tenders and one tablespoon of the sauce, stirring to coat.

2. In a large nonstick skillet with a lid, over medium-high heat, cook the chicken for 3 to 4 minutes until just barely done. Remove the chicken to a plate.

3. Add the vegetables and 1/4 cup of water to the skillet. Cover and cook 4 minutes.

4. Add the remaining sauce and the cooked chicken, mixing well. Cook an additional 3 minutes and serve.

The Asian foods section of your grocery store will have a nice selection of stir-fry sauces. We favor the sesame-ginger.

Look for the fresh and already cut mixed vegetable packages in your produce department near the prewashed bagged salads. If you cannot find fresh vegetable mixes, the frozen food section should offer a bountiful supply. Serve over cooked rice or noodles.

Asian Grilled Fish

SERVINGS: 4
PREPARATION TIME: 10 MINUTES
START TO FINISH TIME: 20 MINUTES,
                    PLUS MARINATING TIME

1/4 cup frozen chopped onion

1 tablespoon ground ginger

1 cup soy sauce or tamari

1/4 cup honey

2 tablespoons sesame oil

4 fish steaks (*such as tuna, swordfish, or salmon*)

1. In a large resealable plastic bag, combine all of the ingredients except for the fish, shaking well to mix.

2. Add the fish steaks; turn to coat with the marinade. Refrigerate for a minimum of 1 hour, or up to 8 hours, turning the bag occasionally.

3. When ready to serve, prepare grill to medium heat. Snip a corner of the bag with scissors and drain the marinade into a small saucepan; set aside.

4. Grill the fish 5 to 7 minutes on each side or until desired doneness. Transfer fish to a serving platter.

5. Bring the marinade to a boil over medium-high heat; reduce the heat to low and simmer for 5 minutes. Pour over grilled fish and serve.

Caribbean Shrimp

SERVINGS: 4
PREPARATION TIME: 10 MINUTES
START TO FINISH TIME: 15 MINUTES

1 teaspoon bottled chopped garlic

1 cup frozen chopped onion

1 tablespoon olive oil

1 teaspoon cumin

1 teaspoon paprika

1 teaspoon salt

1 teaspoon pepper

1 (14 1/2-ounce) can diced tomatoes

1/2 cup coconut milk

1/2 cup milk

1 teaspoon dried cilantro

1 pound raw, peeled and deveined shrimp

1. In a large skillet over medium-high heat, cook the garlic and onion in the oil until the onions are tender, about 5 minutes.

2. Add cumin, paprika, salt, pepper, tomatoes, coconut milk, and milk. Heat for about 1 minute, stirring occasionally.

3. Add cilantro and shrimp. Cook over medium heat for 2 minutes until shrimp are pink.

This racy shrimp dish is a favorite to serve when you need a little spice in your life. Be sure to spoon it generously over plain steamed rice to soak up the flavorful sauce. Salad greens tossed with a light, citrus-based dressing balance the meal and cool your palate nicely. You will be ready to limbo by dessert.

If you do not have coconut milk on hand, increase the regular milk to 1 cup and add 1 teaspoon of sugar.

Fish with Tarragon Tomato Sauce

This dish has such a gourmet taste and it is so easy to prepare. On her night to cook while visiting her favorite cousins at Cape Cod, Cynthia tested this dish using salmon steaks and it was divine.

SERVINGS: 4
PREPARATION TIME: 5 MINUTES
START TO FINISH TIME: 30 MINUTES

1 tablespoon butter or margarine

1 cup frozen chopped onion

1 teaspoon bottled chopped garlic

1 (*14 1/2-ounce*) can diced tomatoes

1/2 cup white wine, optional

1 tablespoon dried parsley

1 tablespoon dried chives

2 teaspoons dried tarragon

1/2 teaspoon salt

1/4 teaspoon pepper

1 pound fresh fish fillets, such as cod, haddock, or salmon

1. In a large deep skillet with a cover, over medium-high heat, melt the butter or margarine. Sauté the onion and garlic for 4 to 5 minutes.

2. Add the remaining ingredients, except for the fish, stirring well to mix. Reduce the heat to low and simmer for 15 minutes, stirring often.

3. Add fish fillets, cover, and simmer for another 10 minutes, turning halfway through cooking time.

Grilled Tilapia
with Cilantro Orange Dressing

SERVINGS: 4
PREPARATION TIME: 10 MINUTES
START TO FINISH TIME: 20 MINUTES

2 tablespoons orange juice concentrate

1/2 teaspoon cumin

1/2 cup lightly packed cilantro leaves

1 tablespoon lemon juice

1/4 cup canola oil

1 teaspoon salt, divided

1/8 teaspoon cayenne pepper

4 tilapia fillets (*snapper, halibut, grouper, or salmon can also be used*)

1/8 teaspoon pepper

cooking spray

1. In a blender container, combine the orange juice concentrate, cumin, cilantro, and lemon juice; blend until smooth.

2. With the blender on, add the canola oil in a thin, steady stream. Add 1/2 teaspoon of the salt and the cayenne pepper. Serve at room temperature with the fish, or the sauce can be made ahead and refrigerated. Allow to sit at room temperature for 30 minutes before serving.

3. When ready for dinner, prepare the grill to medium heat. Spray the fish fillets generously with cooking spray. Sprinkle with the remaining salt and pepper. Grill for 5 minutes on each side or to desired doneness. Transfer to a serving platter.

4. Serve the tilapia and pass the dressing.

Tilapia is a mild, flaky white fish that has found its place on many market fish counters. It is firm enough to place directly on the grill, but be careful not to overcook it; you may lose some of the fish into the flames. To be safe, you can line your grill rack with heavy-duty aluminum foil or use a grill basket.

Cilantro is one of the few herbs with soft, edible, and flavorful stems. In essence, it is the perfect herb for the one-armed cook who does not have the resources to separate and chop fresh herbs.

The versatile dressing we have chosen to accompany the fish is among our favorites. Its zesty flavor and striking green color add a perfect finish to any fish or seafood.

Red-Sauced Linguini with Clams

White wine and artichoke hearts update this traditional favorite.

SERVINGS: 4
PREPARATION TIME: 5 MINUTES
START TO FINISH TIME: 25 MINUTES

1 (*16-ounce*) package linguini

2 teaspoons bottled minced garlic

2 tablespoons olive oil

1/3 cup dry white wine

1 (*26-ounce*) jar pasta sauce

1 (*10-ounce*) package frozen artichoke hearts, defrosted

1 (*10-ounce*) can chopped clams, undrained

2 teaspoons dried basil

1 teaspoon dried parsley

1. In a large pot of lightly salted boiling water, cook linguini according to package directions, drain, and set aside in a serving bowl.

2. In a large saucepan over medium-high heat, sauté the garlic in the oil for 1 minute.

3. Add the wine, pasta sauce, artichokes, and clams. Reduce the heat to low and simmer for 5 minutes. Add the basil and parsley, stirring well to mix.

4. Pour sauce over the pasta and toss well to mix.

Sauteed Scallops
with Lemon and Ginger

SERVINGS: 2
PREPARATION TIME: 5 MINUTES
START TO FINISH TIME: 10 MINUTES

1 tablespoon oil

3 tablespoons butter or margarine, divided

1 pound sea scallops

3 tablespoons lemon juice

1 teaspoon ground ginger

1/2 teaspoon salt

1/4 teaspoon pepper

1. In a large skillet over medium-high heat, heat the oil and 1 tablespoon of the butter or margarine.

2. Add the scallops and cook for 2 minutes, stirring occasionally.

3. Add the lemon juice and cook for 1 more minute.

4. Lower the heat to medium and add the remaining butter or margarine, ginger, salt, and pepper, stirring gently for 1 minute to form a sauce.

The delicately seasoned sauce is a wonderful treatment for scallops. Put the rest of your meal on the table and the scallops will be ready before everything else gets cold.

Seasoned Baked Fish

This is a light and tasty entree. The sauce helps to keep the fish moist.

SERVINGS: 4
PREPARATION TIME: 5 MINUTES
START TO FINISH TIME: 17 MINUTES

1 pound fish fillets, (*such as tilapia or orange roughy*)

2 tablespoons mayonnaise or salad dressing

1/2 teaspoon dried Italian seasoning

1/2 teaspoon salt

1/4 teaspoon pepper

1. Preheat the oven to 400 degrees.

2. Coat a 9 x 13-inch baking dish with cooking spray and place the fish fillets in the baking dish.

3. In a small mixing bowl, combine the remaining ingredients, stirring well to mix; brush over the fillets.

4. Bake for 10 to 12 minutes, or until desired doneness.

Shrimp, Orzo, and Broccoli

SERVINGS: 4
PREPARATION TIME: 10 MINUTES
START TO FINISH TIME: 25 MINUTES

2-1/2 cups chicken broth

1 (*14 1/2-ounce*) can diced tomatoes

1 (*12-ounce*) package fresh chopped broccoli florets

1 cup uncooked orzo

1 pound raw, peeled and deveined shrimp

1 teaspoon salt

1/2 teaspoon pepper

1/4 cup feta cheese, crumbled

2 teaspoons dried basil

1. In a large skillet with a lid, over medium-high heat, combine chicken broth, tomatoes, and broccoli and bring to a boil.

2. Stir in orzo and cover the skillet. Reduce the heat to low and simmer for 7 minutes until orzo is tender.

3. Add shrimp, salt, and pepper, and return to simmer. Cover again, stirring occasionally for 4 more minutes until the shrimp turn pink.

4. Remove skillet from the heat and add the feta cheese and basil, stirring until the cheese is soft.

This easy one-pot meal is also a lovely party dish. Use a large paella pan and double the recipe to serve 8.

Tomato Cream Shrimp
in Pastry Shells

When you're in the mood to serve something a little special, try this shrimp dish. It has such an elegant presentation, but is truly easy on the cook.

SERVINGS: 6
PREPARATION TIME: 20 MINUTES
START TO FINISH TIME: 30 MINUTES

1 (*10-ounce*) package frozen puff pastry shells

2 tablespoons butter or margarine

1/2 cup frozen chopped onion

1 teaspoon bottled minced garlic

1/4 cup flour

2 cups milk

1 (*14 1/2-ounce*) can Italian-style diced tomatoes, drained

1 teaspoon salt

1/4 teaspoon pepper

1 pound raw, peeled and deveined shrimp

1. Preheat oven and bake pastry shells according to package directions and set aside.

2. In a large skillet over medium-high heat, melt the butter or margarine. Add the onions and garlic and cook until the onions are tender, about 5 minutes.

3. Add flour, stirring to coat the onions and garlic.

4. Add the milk, tomatoes, basil, salt, and pepper. Bring to a boil, then reduce heat to low and simmer for 5 minutes, stirring occasionally.

5. Add the shrimp and cook for 2 minutes, stirring until the shrimp turn pink.

6. Spoon shrimp mixture into warm shells.

Ginger-Sherry Lamb Chops

SERVINGS: 2
PREPARATION TIME: 5 MINUTES
START TO FINISH TIME: 25 MINUTES,
                              PLUS MARINATING TIME

1/4 cup soy sauce or tamari

1/4 cup dry sherry

1 teaspoon bottled chopped garlic

1 teaspoon Dijon-style mustard

1 teaspoon ginger

4 lamb chops

1. In a large resealable plastic bag, combine all the ingredients except for the lamb chops, shaking well to mix.

2. Add the lamb chops; turn to coat with the marinade. Refrigerate 4 hours or overnight, turning the bag occasionally.

3. Before cooking the chops, snip a corner of the plastic bag with scissors and drain the marinade into a small saucepan; set aside.

4. **To Broil**: Preheat the broiler. On a foil-lined broiling pan, place the chops and broil on the highest oven rack for 10 minutes on each side or to desired doneness.

5. **To Grill**: Prepare the grill to medium heat. Cook for 10 minutes on each side or to desired doneness.

6. Bring the marinade to a boil over medium-high heat; reduce the heat to low and simmer for 5 minutes. Serve with the lamb chops.

Lamb chops are so easy to prepare. They can be the star of an elegant meal for company, or a romantic dinner for two. Depending on the weather or your mood, these lamb chops can be broiled or grilled. We have included instructions for both.

Rack of Lamb for Two

Believe it or not, you'll soon be ready for a romantic meal for just you and your partner. Babysitters can be hard to find, so don't let that stop you from occasionally treating yourselves to a special meal at home.

This rack of lamb is a classic culinary way to say, "I love you."

SERVINGS: 2
PREPARATION TIME: 10 MINUTES
START TO FINISH TIME: 40 MINUTES

1 (*1- to 1 1/2-pound*) rack of lamb (*about 8 chops*)

1 teaspoon dried whole rosemary leaves

1 teaspoon bottled chopped garlic

2 tablespoons Dijon-style mustard

2 tablespoons olive oil

1 teaspoon salt

1 teaspoon black pepper

1. Preheat the oven to 400 degrees.

2. On a foil-lined baking sheet, place the rack of lamb fat side up.

3. In a small mixing bowl, combine the remaining ingredients, stirring well to mix. Brush this mixture on the lamb.

4. Bake for 30 minutes. Slice the rack between the bones into 8 chops, four for each of you.

Roast Leg of Lamb

SERVINGS: 8
PREPARATION TIME: 10 MINUTES
START TO FINISH TIME: 2 HOURS, 45 MINUTES,
PLUS MARINATING TIME

1 cup dry red wine

1/4 cup lemon juice

1/2 cup olive oil

1 teaspoon dried parsley

1 teaspoon dried thyme

2 teaspoons bottled chopped garlic

1/4 teaspoon nutmeg

1 (6-pound) leg of lamb

4 sprigs fresh rosemary

1. In a 2 1/2-gallon resealable plastic bag, combine the wine, lemon juice, olive oil, parsley, thyme, garlic and nutmeg, shaking well to mix.

2. Add the leg of lamb; turn to coat with the marinade. Refrigerate at least 24 hours and up to 2 days, turning the bag occasionally.

3. When ready to bake, preheat oven to 325 degrees. In a shallow roasting pan, place the leg of lamb. Pour marinade over lamb. Place rosemary sprigs on top of lamb.

4. Bake the lamb for 2-1/2 hours until it reaches an internal temperature of 150 degrees on a meat thermometer. Baste lamb occasionally during roasting.

This is a very upscale main dish for company —and a breeze to cook.

Ham and Cheese Casserole

SERVINGS: 8
PREPARATION TIME: 10 MINUTES
START TO FINISH TIME: 45 MINUTES

Originating from Catherine's grandmother, this recipe is a family favorite. Ask your deli attendant to cut 1/2-inch thick slices of ham or smoked turkey for you, though leftover baked ham works best.

1 (*16-ounce*) package elbow macaroni

1 (*10-ounce*) package frozen peas

2 tablespoons butter or margarine

1 cup frozen chopped onion

1 (*8-ounce*) package fresh sliced mushrooms

1 (*7-ounce*) jar pitted Spanish green olives

1 (*8-ounce*) package shredded Cheddar cheese

1 (*16-ounce*) container sour cream

4 (*1/2-inch*) thick slices boiled ham, baked ham, or smoked turkey (*about 2 pounds*), cut into 1/2-inch cubes

1/2 teaspoon pepper

1/4 cup milk

1/2 cup seasoned breadcrumbs

1. Preheat the oven to 350 degrees.

2. Coat a 2-quart casserole dish with cooking spray.

3. In a large pot of lightly salted water, cook the macaroni according to package directions. When there are about 2 minutes left of cooking time, add the peas to the macaroni. Cook 2 minutes; drain and return to the pot.

4. Meanwhile, in a large skillet over medium-high heat, melt the butter or margarine. Add the onion and mushrooms and cook until the vegetables are tender, about 5 minutes.

5. In the pot with the macaroni and peas, add the mushroom and onion mixture, the olives, cheese, sour cream, ham or smoked turkey, pepper, and milk, stirring well to mix.

6. Transfer to the prepared casserole dish; sprinkle with the breadcrumbs.

7. Bake for 30 minutes, uncovered, until lightly browned and bubbling around the edges.

Catherine's family is an olive-loving bunch, so they always add extra. They can easily be omitted if you are not equally enamored of olives, but it would be very disrespectful. Leftovers are delicious for lunch the next day, or they freeze well for up to 3 months.

Orange-Glazed Ham Steak

This glaze makes a delicious crispy, brown coating that compliments the ham exceptionally well.

SERVINGS: 4
PREPARATION TIME: 10 MINUTES
START TO FINISH TIME: 40 MINUTES

1/2 cup orange marmalade

2 tablespoons Dijon-style mustard

2 tablespoons brown sugar

1 ham steak, cut 1-inch thick

1. Preheat the oven to 350 degrees.

2. In a small mixing bowl, combine the marmalade, mustard, and brown sugar, stirring well to mix.

3. Coat a shallow baking dish with cooking spray, and place the ham steak in the dish. Pour the marmalade mixture over it, turning to coat both sides.

4. Bake, uncovered, for 30 minutes, or until glaze is crisp and brown.

Pork Chops
with Blackberry Preserves

SERVINGS: 6
PREPARATION TIME: 5 MINUTES
START TO FINISH TIME: 40 MINUTES

1/4 cup blackberry preserves

1-1/2 tablespoons Dijon-style mustard

1 tablespoon olive oil

6 center-cut pork chops, 1- to 1 1/2-inch thick

1/2 teaspoon salt

1/4 teaspoon pepper

1/3 cup white or red wine vinegar

1. In a small mixing bowl, combine the preserves and the mustard, stirring well to mix. Set aside.

2. In a large nonstick skillet with a lid, heat the oil over medium-high heat. Add the pork chops, sprinkle with salt and pepper, and cook for 3 minutes on each side, or until lightly browned.

3. Spoon the preserve and mustard mixture evenly over the chops.

4. Reduce heat to low, cover, and cook for 15 minutes or to desired doneness. Transfer chops to a plate.

5. Increase heat to medium; add the vinegar to the sauce in the pan and bring to a boil, stirring frequently and scraping up any bits from the bottom of the skillet. Boil for 5 minutes.

6. Return chops to the sauce and simmer an additional 5 minutes, until chops are heated through.

7. Transfer chops to a serving plate and spoon sauce over the top.

Pork chops are a quick and easy main course. Vinegar adds a nice tang to the sweetness of the fruit in this tasty sauce. We like to garnish the prepared chops with fresh blackberries when they're in season.

Red Pepper Pork

SERVINGS: 4
PREPARATION TIME: 5 MINUTES
START TO FINISH TIME: 50 MINUTES

Pork tenderloins are so moist and tender. Even better still, they are so easy to prepare.

This dish has a nice kick to it, so let it be the main flavor for your dinner.

A plain or slightly sweet rice would be a good side dish.

1-1/2 pounds whole pork tenderloins (*2 small*)

2 tablespoons butter or margarine, melted

1 (*10-ounce*) jar red pepper jelly

1/4 cup white vinegar

1. Preheat the oven to 400 degrees.

2. Coat a roasting pan with cooking spray. Place the tenderloins side by side in the pan.

3. Pour the melted butter evenly over each tenderloin. Place in the oven and bake for 20 minutes.

4. In a small mixing bowl, combine the jelly and vinegar. Pour over the tenderloins and bake an additional 20 to 25 minutes or until the thickest part of the tenderloin reaches 160 degrees on a meat thermometer.

5. Remove the meat from the oven. Place the tenderloins on a platter. Pour the sauce from the pan into a serving bowl.

6. Let the meat rest for 10 minutes before slicing and pass the sauce.

Southwestern Pork Chops

SERVINGS: 6
PREPARATION TIME: 10 MINUTES
START TO FINISH TIME: 25 MINUTES

1 cup prepared chunky tomato salsa

1 (*15-ounce*) can whole corn, drained

1 (*15-ounce*) can black beans, rinsed and drained

1 teaspoon vegetable oil

6 pork loin chops

1. In a medium mixing bowl, combine the salsa, corn, and black beans, stirring well to mix.

2. In a large skillet with a lid, heat the oil over medium-high heat. Add the pork chops and brown on one side for 4 minutes.

3. Turn chops over and spoon the salsa mixture evenly over the top.

4. Reduce the heat to low, cover and simmer the pork chops for 8 to 10 minutes or to desired doneness.

Top these chops with shredded cheddar cheese and sprigs of fresh cilantro. Serve them with cornbread and some applesauce to balance the spiciness.

Sweet and Sour Pork Chops

The fruity undertones of apple cider make this a special dish.

SERVINGS: 2
PREPARATION TIME: 10 MINUTES
START TO FINISH TIME: 30 MINUTES

1 tablespoon olive oil

2 (*1-inch*) thick pork rib chops

1/2 teaspoon salt

1/4 teaspoon pepper

1 cup apple cider

2 tablespoons light brown sugar, packed

2 tablespoons apple cider vinegar

1/2 teaspoon mustard seeds

1. In a large skillet over medium-high heat, heat the oil. Add the pork chops, sprinkle with salt and pepper, and cook for 4 minutes on each side, until browned.

2. In a small mixing bowl, combine the apple cider and the brown sugar, stirring well to mix. Add to the skillet, and bring to a boil. Simmer, uncovered, for 5 minutes, turning chops once. Transfer chops to a plate.

3. Add vinegar and mustard seeds to sauce in the pan and return to a boil. Simmer, uncovered, for 5 minutes, stirring often to scrape up any bits from the bottom of the skillet.

4. Return chops to the sauce and simmer for an additional 5 minutes, until chops are heated through and sauce is slightly thickened.

5. Transfer chops to a serving plate and spoon glaze over the top.

Slow Cooking

Although we mentioned in the bread chapter that a bread machine was the kitchen appliance that gave us the most pleasure, the kitchen appliance we could not live without is our slow cooker.

Go out to the garage or up to the attic right now and find that slow cooker you were given as a wedding present or call your Mom to send you hers that she has been saving in a box marked *"garage sale"*. You need this appliance!

In terms of eliminating late afternoon stress, not even a masseuse could do for you what a slow cooker can do. **Put all the ingredients in one pot in the morning and, when you are ready for dinner, dinner is ready for you.**

You, too, can have dinner waiting on you instead of the other way around, but it's easy to make excuses that keep you from doing it. The most common excuse we hear from our friends is that they don't have the time to plan ahead. It really is not as difficult as it seems.

If you are going to the grocery store just once a week, you need to plan for only three meals. Two of the three meals you cook should be made to do double duty—two for the table and two for the freezer that can be defrosted and heated later that week. That leaves one original meal, perhaps to satisfy a craving or special request, and two unplanned meals a week. One may consist of take-out, restaurant dining, or accepting an invitation from friends. The other may be something more spur-of-the-moment, like soup and sandwiches or omelets. Keep bagged lettuce and bottled salad dressing stocked in your refrigerator to round out any meal with a salad.

Late afternoon and early evening can be a wicked time in any household. Plan to take away some of that stress with a few meals from the slow cooker. Better to have some extra time to lie on the floor and coo at the baby than stand over the stove and curse at the pot.

Asian Chicken Drumsticks

SERVINGS: 6
PREPARATION TIME: 10 MINUTES
START TO FINISH TIME: 5 HOURS, 10 MINUTES

1/2 cup soy sauce or tamari

1/3 cup brown sugar

1 teaspoon bottled chopped garlic

1 (*8-ounce*) can tomato sauce

6 skinless chicken drumsticks with thighs attached

1. In the bottom of a 3 1/2-quart, or larger, slow cooker, place all of the ingredients except for the chicken, stirring well to mix.

2. Add chicken; stir to coat with the sauce.

3. Cover and cook on low for 5 hours.

If skinless quarters aren't available, purchase one package of skinless drumsticks and one package of skinless thighs.

There's no need to increase the other ingredients, since this recipe makes enough sauce to cover the few extra pieces.

Beef Shanks
in Tangy Tomato Sauce

Try this low-cost, no-fuss, high-flavor main course in your slow cooker. It is a family favorite.

SERVINGS: 6
PREPARATION TIME: 15 MINUTES
START TO FINISH TIME: 9 HOURS, 15 MINUTES

1 (*12-ounce*) can beer

1 (*6-ounce*) can tomato paste

1 cup frozen chopped onion

1 (*8-ounce*) package sliced fresh mushrooms

1 (*16-ounce*) package fresh baby carrots

1/4 teaspoon salt

1/4 teaspoon pepper

1 heaping tablespoon bottled chopped garlic

2-1/2 pounds beef shanks (*boneless, if available*)

2 tablespoons cornstarch

2 tablespoons water

2 tablespoons lemon juice

1. In the bottom of a 3 1/2-quart, or larger, slow cooker, place beer and tomato paste, stirring well to mix.

2. Add the onion, mushrooms, carrots, salt, pepper, and garlic, stirring well to mix.

3. Add beef shanks; stir to coat with the sauce.

4. Cover and cook on low for 9 hours.

5. Remove beef to a serving platter; cover to keep warm.

6. Turn slow cooker to high. In a small mixing bowl, combine cornstarch and water until smooth. Add cornstarch mixture to sauce, stirring well to mix. Cook an additional 15 minutes until sauce thickens.

7. Stir in lemon juice, pour sauce over beef, and serve.

Chapter Thirteen — Slow Cooking

Beef Stroganoff

SERVINGS: 6
PREPARATION TIME: 10 MINUTES
START TO FINISH TIME: 8 HOURS, 10 MINUTES

1 cup frozen chopped onion

1 teaspoon bottled minced garlic

1 tablespoon Worcestershire sauce

1/4 cup ketchup

1/4 cup red wine

1 (8-ounce) package fresh sliced mushrooms

1-1/2 pounds beef stew meat

1 (8-ounce) carton reduced-fat sour cream

1. In a 3 1/2-quart, or larger, slow cooker, place all of the ingredients except for the beef stew meat and sour cream, stirring well to mix.

2. Add the beef stew meat; stir to coat with the sauce.

3. Cover and cook on low for 8 hours.

4. Stir in sour cream and serve.

Enjoy this old-fashioned favorite slow and easy from the slow cooker. Be sure to select stew meat that has been well trimmed of fat. Serve with hot buttered noodles.

Chicken and Black Olives

This recipe came with Cynthia's slow cooker and it has become a family favorite. Serve with rice.

SERVINGS: 6
PREPARATION TIME: 15 MINUTES
START TO FINISH TIME: 8 HOURS, 15 MINUTES

1/2 cup frozen chopped onion

2 teaspoons bottled minced garlic

1 cup chicken broth

1/2 cup sherry, optional

1 teaspoon Tabasco

1 teaspoon oregano

1/2 teaspoon salt

6 boneless, skinless chicken breasts

1 (3 4/5-ounce) can sliced ripe olives

1. In the bottom of a 3 1/2-quart, or larger, slow cooker, place all of the ingredients except for the chicken and olives, and stir well to mix.

2. Add the chicken; stir to coat with the sauce.

3. Cover and cook on low for 8 hours.

4. Stir in olives and serve.

Italian Pork Chops

SERVINGS: 6
PREPARATION TIME: 15 MINUTES
START TO FINISH TIME: 8 HOURS, 15 MINUTES

1 (8-ounce) package fresh sliced mushrooms

1/2 cup frozen chopped onion

1 teaspoon bottled chopped garlic

1 tablespoon lemon juice

6 lean pork chops, 1-inch thick

1 (26-ounce) jar prepared pasta sauce

1. In the bottom of a 3 1/2-quart, or larger, slow cooker, place the mushrooms, onions, garlic, and lemon juice.

2. Add pork chops.

3. Pour pasta sauce over the pork chops. Cover and cook on low for 8 hours.

This easy one-pot meal can be made with pasta sauce seasoned any way you like. We use a tomato-basil flavored sauce most frequently.

If you have the extra resources, browning the pork chops for 2 minutes on each side in 1 tablespoon of vegetable oil in a medium skillet over medium-high heat before adding them to the pot enhances the flavor of this dish. Either way, the pork will be very tender.

Mexican Chicken

This will satisfy your craving for something Mexican without having to order takeout.

SERVINGS: 4
PREPARATION TIME: 10 MINUTES
START TO FINISH TIME: 5 HOURS, 10 MINUTES

2 cups converted rice

1 (28-ounce) can diced tomatoes

1 (6-ounce) can tomato paste

3 cups hot water

1 envelope taco seasoning mix

1/2 cup frozen chopped onion

1/2 cup frozen chopped green pepper

1 (1 1/2-pound) package boneless and skinless chicken thighs (about 6)

1. In a 3 1/2-quart, or larger, slow cooker, place all of the ingredients except for the chicken, stirring well to mix.

2. Add the chicken; stir to coat with the sauce.

3. Cover and cook on low for 5 hours.

Mock Coq Au Vin

SERVINGS: 6
PREPARATION TIME: 10 MINUTES
START TO FINISH TIME: 5 HOURS, 25 MINUTES

1/3 cup red raspberry jam

1/4 cup red wine

3 tablespoons soy sauce or tamari

1 teaspoon prepared mustard

1 (8-ounce) package sliced mushrooms

1/2 cup frozen chopped onion

12 skinless chicken drumsticks

2 tablespoons cornstarch

2 tablespoons cold water

3 cups cooked rice

1. In the bottom of a 3 1/2-quart, or larger, slow cooker, place the jam, wine, soy sauce or tamari, and mustard, stirring well to mix.

2. Add mushrooms and onion to the mixture, stirring well to mix.

3. Add the chicken; stir to coat with the sauce.

4. Cover and cook on low for 5 hours.

5. Place cooked rice on serving platter. Remove chicken from slow cooker and arrange on top of rice; cover to keep warm.

6. Turn slow cooker to high. In a small mixing bowl, combine cornstarch and water until smooth. Add cornstarch mixture to sauce, stirring well to mix. Cook an additional 15 minutes until sauce thickens.

7. Spoon sauce over chicken and rice and serve.

When Cynthia made this dish for her husband, he said, "Oh honey, this Coq au Vin is delicious!" The recipe was originally titled "Chicken Drumsticks in Raspberry Sauce"— she changed it immediately!

You can prepare the cooked rice during the last hour of cook time for the chicken, or the rice can be prepared ahead, covered, and refrigerated for up to 3 days.

To reheat, place the rice in a microwave-safe dish and add a little water to create steam so the rice does not dry out. Place the dish in a microwave oven and cook on high for 2 minutes, stirring occasionally, until the rice is heated through.

Pot Roast
with Lime Tomato Sauce

SERVINGS: 4
PREPARATION TIME: 5 MINUTES
START TO FINISH TIME: 8 HOURS, 35 MINUTES,
PLUS MARINATING TIME

Comfort foods are, of course, different for everyone, but in Cynthia's family, this recipe is a universal favorite. Every time she serves it, her family feels loved.

If you only have lemon juice on hand, make it with that -- it will still be tasty.

1 tablespoon bottled minced garlic

1/3 cup lime juice

1 (*3-pound*) chuck roast

1 (*14 1/2-ounce*) can beef broth

1 teaspoon Italian seasoning

1 (*28-ounce*) can crushed tomatoes

2 tablespoons cornstarch

2 tablespoons cold water

1. In a large resealable plastic bag, place the garlic and the lime juice.

2. Add the roast; turn to coat with the marinade. Refrigerate overnight, turning the bag occasionally.

3. When ready to slow cook, place the roast in a 3 1/2-quart, or larger, slow cooker; discard the marinade

4. Add the broth, seasoning, and tomatoes.

5. Cover the pot, and cook on low for 8 hours.

6. Remove the roast to a serving platter; cover to keep warm.

7. Turn slow cooker to high. In a small mixing bowl, combine cornstarch and water until smooth. Add cornstarch mixture to sauce, stirring well to mix. Cook an additional 15 minutes until sauce thickens.

8. Pour the sauce over the roast and serve.

Chapter Thirteen — Slow Cooking

Meatless Main Dishes

14

Many of us, whether motivated by health concerns or budgetary constraints, have already embraced the idea of meatless meals. However, many so-called *"vegetarian"* recipes are notoriously laden with high-fat dairy products and are, ironically, devoid of vegetables.

The recipes we have chosen feature a more healthful array of vegetables, legumes, pasta, rice, grains, nuts, dairy products, and tofu. While many of our recipes are low in fat, we have also included some of the aforementioned *"richer"* dairy selections for your occasional indulgence that we guarantee will be worth those extra miles with the jog stroller.

At this unique time in your life, perhaps a more important consideration than fat content is protein. While recovering from pregnancy, healing from childbirth, and adjusting to a new life with baby, your body needs extra protein (*and you need NOT consume a side-of-beef in order to meet these requirements!*). Tofu and combinations of legumes and whole grains, the main ingredients in most of our recipes, provide efficient and complete proteins, while lending you more fiber, more energy, and less fat in the process. They are also very easy on your pocketbook.

Most large chain supermarkets will carry all the items you need to complete our recipes. If you have trouble finding an ingredient, ask the store manager (*for example, Catherine's mother lives in a rural community and she could not find tofu in her two local grocery stores*). It may be stocked in an unlikely place or not stocked at all. Many grocers are eager to please customers with special requests. If you must venture to a health food store or specialty market, we recommend you stock up.

All of our recipes prove that a meal without meat need not be defunct of flavor or fun. **We offer a broad range of innovative main dishes, redolent of spices and full of flavor that should satisfy even the most devout carnivore.** We hope you discover that *"eating your vegetables"* is not only good for you, but just plain good!

Cold Bean and Artichoke Salad

SERVINGS: 8
PREPARATION TIME: 5 MINUTES
START TO FINISH TIME: 15 MINUTES

1 (*15-ounce*) can Great Northern beans
    or other white beans, drained

1 (*15-ounce*) can chickpeas, drained

1 (*15-ounce*) can black beans, drained

1 (*14-ounce*) can artichoke heart quarters, drained

1 (*14 1/2-ounce*) can diced tomatoes, drained

1 tablespoon bottled minced garlic

1/4 cup olive oil

1/4 cup balsamic vinegar

2 teaspoons dried oregano

1 teaspoon pepper

1. In a large mixing bowl, combine all the ingredients, stirring well to mix.

2. Refrigerate for at least 1 hour, or preferably 1 day, before serving.

If you are under the impression that bean salads are old—fashioned, just take a bite of this one.

The addition of artichokes (and plenty of garlic) makes this salad a modern classic. This recipe doubles and triples easily and is a great choice for "toting". Serve this salad over a bed of leaf lettuce for lunch or as a light supper. The leftovers taste even better.

Gourmet Fried Rice

Next time you make a pot of steamed rice, make extra for the refrigerator or freezer and you will have the foundation for this fabulous recipe. Quick and flavorful, it takes a turn from the traditional Chinese version of fried rice.

SERVINGS: 4
PREPARATION TIME: 10 MINUTES
START TO FINISH TIME: 20 MINUTES

1 (*10-ounce*) package frozen green beans, cut or Italian-style flat beans

1/4 cup olive oil

1 cup frozen chopped onion

1 tablespoon bottled chopped garlic

1 teaspoon cumin

1 teaspoon tumeric

1 pinch crushed red pepper

3 cups cold cooked rice

1-1/2 teaspoons salt

1 (*14 1/2-ounce*) can diced tomatoes, drained

1 (*15-ounce*) can artichoke quarters, drained

1 (*15-ounce*) can white kidney beans, rinsed and drained

1/3 cup toasted, unsalted sunflower seed kernels or hulled pumpkin seeds

1. Cook the frozen green beans according to package directions, omitting salt. Drain and set aside.

2. Meanwhile, in a large skillet over medium-high heat, heat the olive oil. Add onion and garlic, and cook until tender, about 5 minutes.

3. Add cumin, tumeric, and crushed red pepper. Cook for 2 minutes to release flavors, stirring frequently.

4. Add the rice, crumbling it, and the salt. Cook, stirring frequently, until the rice begins to turn golden brown, about 3 minutes.

5. Add the cooked green beans, tomatoes, artichoke hearts, and white kidney beans and cook for 2 minutes, stirring until heated through.

6. Remove from heat and sprinkle with sunflower seed kernels or hulled pumpkin seeds.

This dish benefits from reheating, so it's a great do-ahead one.

Be sure to reheat it in a skillet on the stovetop over medium heat, stirring frequently.

Grilled Tofu

SERVINGS: 6
PREPARATION TIME: 10 MINUTES
START TO FINISH TIME: 20 MINUTES,
                        PLUS MARINATING TIME

2 (*16-ounce*) containers extra-firm tofu

1/4 cup canola oil

1/3 cup prepared barbeque sauce

1/3 cup peanut butter

2 teaspoons bottled minced garlic

1. Rinse the tofu bricks with water and drain in a colander while you prepare the marinade.

2. In a medium mixing bowl, combine the remaining ingredients, mixing well with a wire whisk.

3. Slice each brick of tofu into 6 equal-sized slabs and place in a shallow pan.

4. Brush the marinade over the tofu, turning to coat both sides. Marinate for at least 1 hour.

5. When ready to cook, coat the grill with cooking spray and prepare the grill to medium heat. Cook tofu for 5 minutes on each side or until lightly charred and heated through.

To Broil or Bake:

When you do not feel like braving the elements
to fire up the grill, broiling yields similar results.
Simply line a baking sheet with aluminum foil, coat
it with cooking spray, and arrange the tofu on the
prepared sheet. Broil on the highest rack closest to the
broiler for 5 minutes on each side or until lightly brown
and heated through.

You can also bake this tofu. Preheat the oven to
350 degrees. Coat a 9 x 13-inch baking dish with
cooking spray, and place tofu in a single layer in
the dish. Bake for 30 minutes, turning tofu halfway
through cooking time.

*Catherine's close
friend, Caryn, is
renowned for her
version of this recipe.
Even our friends who
are not particularly
fond of tofu LOVE it
prepared this way.*

*Leftovers are great on
sandwiches and atop
salads and baked
potatoes.*

*For an easy variation,
simply brush your
favorite marinade on
the tofu slabs and cook
according to the
directions that follow.
Teriyaki sauce and
sesame-ginger
dressing are among
our favorites.*

Lentil Spaghetti

This hearty vegetarian "Bolognese" is very satisfying. Serve it with a bagged Italian blend of mixed greens tossed with a good quality bottled Caesar salad dressing and plenty of croutons.

SERVINGS: 4
PREPARATION TIME: 5 MINUTES
START TO FINISH TIME: 20 MINUTES

1 (*16-ounce*) box spaghetti

1 tablespoon olive oil

1 cup frozen chopped onions

1 teaspoon bottled minced garlic

2 cups favorite prepared pasta sauce

2 (*15-ounce*) cans lentils, rinsed and drained

Grated Parmesan cheese, optional

1. In a large pot of lightly salted boiling water, cook the spaghetti according to package directions. Drain and set aside.

2. Meanwhile, in a large skillet over medium-high heat, heat the olive oil. Add the onions and garlic and cook until the onions are tender, about 5 minutes.

3. Stir in the pasta sauce and lentils; reduce the heat to low and simmer for 10 minutes.

4. Serve over spaghetti and sprinkle with the Parmesan cheese, if desired.

Lentil and Rice Casserole

SERVINGS: 6
PREPARATION TIME: 10 MINUTES
START TO FINISH TIME: 2 HOURS, 10 MINUTES

1 cup uncooked brown rice

1 cup dried lentils

1 cup frozen chopped onion

1 (*32-ounce*) container vegetable broth

1 tablespoon dried Italian seasoning

1 teaspoon salt

1/2 teaspoon garlic powder

1 (*8-ounce*) package shredded Cheddar cheese

1. Preheat the oven to 350 degrees.

2. Coat a 1 1/2-quart casserole dish with cooking spray.

3. In a large mixing bowl, combine all the ingredients, stirring well to mix.

4. Pour into the prepared dish.

5. Bake, covered, 1-1/2 to 2 hours.

This dish always appears on the menu when there is a mixed crowd of carnivores and herbivores. The meat-eaters love it as a side dish, and the vegetarians heap it onto their plates as a satisfying main dish. The cheese can be omitted without compromising the success of this recipe.

Nutty Thai Noodles

Asian cooking is so popular and this recipe gives you the hint of Asian flavors, with no fuss. Our **Broccoli Slaw Salad** is a perfect companion to add color to your plate and round out the meal. We also like this dish with any grilled meat.

If you coat your measuring cup with cooking spray, the peanut butter glides out without sticking.

1 (*16-ounce*) box vermicelli, or thin spaghetti

2 tablespoons rice vinegar

1/4 cup soy sauce or tamari

2 tablespoons sesame oil

1/3 cup chunky peanut butter

2 teaspoons bottled minced garlic

1/2 teaspoon red pepper flakes

1 teaspoon ground ginger

1. In a large pot of lightly salted boiling water, cook the vermicelli according to package directions. Drain and place in a serving bowl.

2. In a large microwave-safe bowl or measuring cup, combine the remaining ingredients to make the sauce, stirring well to mix.

3. Cook the sauce for 1 minute on half power in the microwave.

4. Pour warm sauce over the vermicelli and toss to coat.

Pasta Putanesca

SERVINGS: 4
PREPARATION TIME: 10 MINUTES
START TO FINISH TIME: 25 MINUTES

1 (16-ounce) box linguini

1/4 cup olive oil

1 (4 1/2-ounce) can sliced black olives

1 (8-ounce) jar oil-packed sun-dried tomatoes, drained

1 (3-ounce) jar capers, drained

1 heaping tablespoon bottled chopped garlic

1/2 teaspoon crushed red pepper

1 teaspoon oregano

1 (28-ounce) can diced tomatoes

1/4 cup prepared pesto

Grated Parmesan cheese, optional

1. In a large pot of lightly salted boiling water, cook the linguini according to package directions. Drain and set aside.

2. Meanwhile, in a large skillet over medium heat, add the olive oil, olives, sun-dried tomatoes, capers, garlic, crushed red pepper, and oregano, stirring well to mix. Cook for 5 minutes.

3. Add the diced tomatoes and the pesto, stirring well to mix. Cook for an additional 10 minutes, or until the sauce has thickened to your liking

4. Serve hot over the cooked linguini. Sprinkle with Parmesan cheese, if desired, and enjoy!

Prepare this dish for your "foody" friends who will truly appreciate all the intense flavors. Be sure to serve it with some crusty bread to sop up every drop. Leftover sauce is wonderful on grilled chicken or fish.

If you can make the sauce the day before, it improves overnight in the refrigerator. Gently reheat it in a saucepan or in the microwave while the pasta is cooking.

Pasta with Broccoli and 'Shrooms
in Garlic Wine Sauce

Servings: 4
Preparation Time: 10 minutes
Start to Finish Time: 30 minutes

Garlic and white wine offer this recipe distinctive flavor with elegant results.

1 (*16-ounce*) box angel hair pasta

1/4 cup butter or margarine

1/4 cup olive oil

1 cup frozen chopped onions

1 tablespoon bottled minced garlic

1 (*10-ounce*) package frozen broccoli florets

1 (*8-ounce*) package fresh sliced mushrooms

1/2 cup dry white wine

1/2 cup grated Parmesan cheese

1. In a large pot of lightly salted boiling water, cook the pasta according to package directions. Drain and transfer to a serving dish.

2. Meanwhile, in a large skillet over medium-high heat, melt the butter or margarine; add the olive oil, stirring well to mix.

3. Add the onions and cook until tender, about 5 minutes.

4. Reduce the heat to medium. Add the garlic, broccoli, and mushrooms and continue cooking, stirring occasionally, an additional 10 minutes, or until the broccoli is desired tenderness.

5. Add the wine; simmer uncovered, for 5 minutes.

6. Pour the sauce over the pasta; sprinkle with the Parmesan cheese; toss well to mix.

Pasta with Creamy Tomato
and Goat Cheese Sauce

SERVINGS: 4
PREPARATION TIME: 5 MINUTES
START TO FINISH TIME: 15 MINUTES

1 (*16-ounce*) box farfalle or rotini pasta

2 cups favorite prepared pasta sauce

1 (*4-ounce*) log goat cheese, cut into 4 pieces

1. In a large pot of lightly salted boiling water, cook the pasta according to package directions. Drain and transfer to a serving dish.

2. In a small saucepan over medium heat, heat the pasta sauce for 5 to 10 minutes, or until lightly bubbling, stirring occasionally.

3. Reduce the heat to low. Add the goat cheese to the pasta sauce and stir until melted and smooth.

4. Pour the hot sauce over the pasta; toss to coat.

When you are really challenged for time, nothing beats this pasta dish for flavor and quickness. The goat cheese melts easily into the pasta sauce elevating a normally satisfying dish to a divine one.
Adding a package of frozen chopped spinach to the pasta during the last few minutes of boiling would add a nice nutritional and colorful boost.

Quick-Fix Pizzas

SERVINGS: 4
PREPARATION TIME: 10 MINUTES
START TO FINISH TIME: 20 MINUTES

4 (6-inch) Italian bread shells

4 tablespoons olive oil, divided

1 cup prepared marinara sauce, divided

1 (8-ounce) package shredded mozzarella cheese, divided

4 tablespoons grated Parmesan cheese, divided

1 teaspoon oregano, divided

1. Preheat the oven to 450 degrees.

2. Coat a baking sheet with cooking spray. Place the bread shells on the prepared baking sheet.

3. Brush each bread shell with 1 tablespoon of olive oil.

4. Spread 1/4 cup of the marinara evenly over each bread shell, then sprinkle each evenly with 1/2 cup of the Mozzarella cheese, 1 tablespoon of the Parmesan cheese, and 1 pinch of oregano.

5. Bake for 8 to 10 minutes, until the cheese is melted and lightly browned around the edges.

Sauce variations: Substitute 1 tablespoon of prepared pesto per pizza for the marinara; or add 1 additional tablespoon of olive oil with 1/2 teaspoon of bottled minced garlic per pizza, and omit the marinara.

Cheese variations: Decrease the amount of mozzarella and add Cheddar, ricotta, Gorgonzola, goat cheese, or feta cheese to your taste.

Borrow ideas from your favorite pizzeria or let your imagination run wild. Built with healthful ingredients, pizza makes a fast and balanced main meal. Or slice them into smaller wedges and you have extraordinary appetizers or snacks for a crowd.

Topping variations: This is where creative cooks can have lots of fun. Our personal favorites are fresh basil leaves, sun-dried tomatoes, roasted red peppers, marinated artichoke hearts (*drained*), fresh baby spinach, fresh sliced mushrooms, or our **Grilled Portobello Mushrooms**, and sliced green and black olives.

Meat-lovers can raid the deli and prepared-food sections of their supermarkets for pepperoni, salami, prosciutto, and cooked chicken.

Be sure to check your refrigerator for any tasty remnants from previous meals, like cooked vegetables, meats, poultry, and seafood. It is a great way to use up even small amounts of leftovers.

Tofu Marinara

This is one of our favorite ways to enjoy tofu. It is so chunky and flavorful; you can really sink your teeth into this meal and not feel meat-deprived. It stands alone next to a tossed salad; or try it generously spooned over pasta, rice, or a baked potato.

SERVINGS: 4
PREPARATION TIME: 15 MINUTES
START TO FINISH TIME: 35 MINUTES

2 tablespoons olive oil

1 cup frozen chopped onion

1 cup frozen chopped bell pepper

1 (8-ounce) package fresh sliced mushrooms

1 teaspoon bottled minced garlic

1 (16-ounce) container extra-firm tofu, rinsed and drained, and cut into 1-inch cubes, or crumbled with your hand

1 teaspoon salt

1 (15 3/4-ounce) jar prepared pasta sauce

1/2 cup grated Parmesan cheese

1. In a large skillet over medium-high heat, heat the olive oil. Add the onion, pepper, and mushrooms and cook until the vegetables are tender, about 10 minutes.

2. Add the garlic, tofu, and salt; continue cooking for 2 minutes, stirring frequently.

3. Add the pasta sauce, stirring well to mix.

4. Reduce heat to low and simmer, covered, for 10 minutes.

5. Remove from heat. Add the Parmesan cheese, stirring well to mix.

Tortellini
with Broccoli and Artichokes

SERVINGS: 6
PREPARATION TIME: 10 MINUTES
START TO FINISH TIME: 30 MINUTES

3 (8-ounce) packages fresh or frozen tortellini

1/2 cup butter or margarine

1 (10-ounce) package frozen broccoli florets, defrosted

1 (8-ounce) package fresh sliced mushrooms

1 (14-ounce) can artichoke heart quarters, drained

1 cup half-and-half

1 (4 1/2-ounce) can sliced black olives, drained

1 cup shredded Italian cheese blend

1 cup grated Parmesan cheese

1/4 teaspoon pepper

1. In a large pot of lightly salted boiling water, cook the tortellini according to package directions. Drain and set aside.

2. Meanwhile, in a large skillet over medium-high heat, melt the butter or margarine. Add the broccoli and mushrooms, and cook until the vegetables are tender, about 5 minutes.

3. Add the artichoke quarters and half-and-half. Cook, stirring constantly, for 5 minutes or until slightly thickened.

4. Add the black olives, cheeses, and pepper; stir until the cheeses are melted.

5. Reduce the heat to low. Add the tortellini, and cook for 2 minutes, stirring gently, until heated through.

When Catherine was a newlywed and just starting to entertain, this recipe was a staple. You can even stir in cooked boneless chicken pieces for a "non-vegetarian" crowd.

Italian cheese blend may be packaged with different names, depending on the brand. Usually, it is a mixture of cheeses consisting primarily of mozzarella and provolone with the addition of Parmesan, Romano, and sometimes Asiago cheeses.

Vegetarian Chili

Our **Snacking Corn Bread** is the perfect companion to this hearty chili.
You can adjust the amount of chili powder and cumin according to your tolerance.
Serve the individual bowls of chili with shredded sharp Cheddar cheese, a dollop of sour cream, and/or a scoop of leftover rice on top.

SERVINGS: 6
PREPARATION TIME: 10 MINUTES
START TO FINISH TIME: 35 MINUTES

2 tablespoons vegetable oil

1 (*10-ounce*) package frozen chopped onions

1 (*10-ounce*) package frozen chopped bell pepper

1 tablespoon bottled minced garlic

1/4 cup chili powder

1 tablespoon cumin

1 teaspoon salt

2 (*14 1/2-ounce*) cans Mexican-style stewed tomatoes

1 (*15-ounce*) can lentils, rinsed and drained

1 (*15-ounce*) can red kidney beans or pinto beans, rinsed and drained

1 (*15 1/4-ounce*) can whole kernel corn, drained

1. In a large pot over medium heat, heat the vegetable oil. Add the onion, pepper, and garlic, and cook until tender, about 10 minutes.

2. Add the chili powder, cumin, and salt, stirring well to mix. Cook for 2 minutes to release flavors, stirring frequently.

3. Add the tomatoes, lentils, kidney beans or pinto beans, and corn, stirring well to mix.

4. Bring to a boil, cover, reduce the heat to low, and simmer for 10 minutes.

178

Vegetable Side Dishes

When deciding on side dishes to accompany the main entree, we not only consider what will taste good, but also what will look good on the plate. A vibrant burst of green, orange, or red can make drab brown meat and potatoes more exciting to both the eye and the palate. The added nutritional value goes without saying.

Nature demonstrates both artistry and generosity by providing us vegetables and fruits in every color of the spectrum. Equally diverse are their flavors and textures, which offer a range of sensations. The balance you strike between these elements on the same plate can be dramatic and make a mediocre meal spectacular.

We find that cooking vegetables on the stovetop or in the microwave requires approximately the same amount of time, attention, and labor to make them recipe-ready. Therefore, we have left the decision up to you, except where a specific cooking method is called for to ensure a desired outcome.

We enjoy our veggies crisp-tender, versus the mushy presentation we both grew up with, so watch your cooking time and adjust it according to your preference. Omit salt during cooking, because we have suggested its addition later in the recipes.

Asian Noodle-Rice Casserole

SERVINGS: 12
PREPARATION TIME: 10 MINUTES
START TO FINISH TIME: 30 MINUTES

This is a great recipe to serve a crowd. It was critically acclaimed by all of our children. This dish can be prepared ahead, covered, and refrigerated for up to 3 days.

To reheat, place the noodle-rice in a microwave-safe serving dish and add a little water to create steam so it does not dry out. Place the dish in a microwave oven and cook on high for 5 minutes, stirring occasionally until heated through. It also freezes well for up to 3 months.

1 stick butter or margarine

1 (*12-ounce*) package thin egg noodles

1 (*32-ounce*) container chicken broth

1 cup water

1 (*10 1/2-ounce*) can French onion soup

3 cups instant rice

1 (*8-ounce*) can sliced water chestnuts

1 (*8-ounce*) package fresh sliced mushrooms

1 tablespoon soy sauce or tamari

1. In a large pot over medium-high heat, melt the butter or margarine.

2. Add the noodles and cook, stirring often, until golden brown, about 5 minutes.

3. Add the chicken broth, water, and French onion soup, stirring well to mix. Increase the heat to high and bring liquids to a boil.

4. Add the remaining ingredients, stirring well to mix.

5. Reduce heat to low, cover, and simmer, stirring occasionally, until liquid is absorbed, about 10 minutes.

Chapter Fifteen — Vegetable Side Dishes

Broccoli Slaw Salad

SERVINGS: 8
PREPARATION TIME: 15 MINUTES
START TO FINISH TIME: 15 MINUTES, PLUS 6 HOURS FOR
MARINATING

1/2 cup sugar

1/2 cup white vinegar

1/2 cup canola oil

2 (3-ounce) packages beef flavor ramen noodles,
    flavor packets reserved

1 (16-ounce) package broccoli slaw

1/2 cup sliced almonds

1/2 cup sunflower seed kernels

1 (15-ounce) can Mandarin oranges, drained

1. In a large resealable plastic bag, combine the sugar,
   vinegar, oil, and reserved beef flavor packets,
   shaking well to mix.

2. Add the broccoli slaw, shaking well to coat with
   the dressing.

3. Break the ramen noodles apart by hand into bite-sized
   pieces over the broccoli slaw. Shake well to mix
   the noodles and slaw with the dressing.

4. Refrigerate for at least 6 hours, shaking the bag
   occasionally to mix the salad.

5. Just before serving, transfer the salad to a serving
   bowl. Add the remaining ingredients; toss well to mix.

This recipe found a permanent place in Catherine's repertoire after a Little League championship celebration. It has become her favorite salad to bring to picnics and potluck gatherings. It is always the first dish to empty and is one of her most requested recipes.

If broccoli slaw is not available, you can substitute cabbage slaw with similar results. It must be made at least 6 hours before serving, so plan accordingly.

If you have trouble breaking the noodles apart by hand, they can be put into another resealable plastic bag, broken into bite-sized pieces with a meat-tenderizing mallet or a rolling pin, and added to the broccoli slaw mixture.

Broccoli with Water Chestnuts

SERVINGS: 8
PREPARATION TIME: 5 MINUTES
START TO FINISH TIME: 13 MINUTES

2 (*10-ounce*) packages frozen chopped broccoli, defrosted

1 (*8-ounce*) can sliced or chopped water chestnuts, drained

1 cup chopped pecans

2 tablespoons butter or margarine

1/4 cup grated Parmesan cheese

1/2 cup cracker crumbs

1/4 cup chicken, beef, or vegetable broth

2 tablespoons dried onion

1. In a large microwave-safe serving dish, combine all the ingredients, stirring well to mix.

2. Cover dish and cook on high for 5 to 8 minutes, stirring every 2 minutes, until broccoli is cooked to desired tenderness.

You can make fresh cracker crumbs for this recipe very easily by placing about 10 "Ritz"-style crackers in a resealable plastic bag and pounding them with your fist. (It's also a great stress reducer.) One time, all Catherine had on hand were cheddar cheese crackers (about 30), and the results were phenomenal.

Cauliflower
with Tomatoes and Feta Cheese

SERVINGS: 4
PREPARATION TIME: 5 MINUTES
START TO FINISH TIME: 20 MINUTES

3 tablespoons olive oil

1 cup frozen chopped onions

1 teaspoon bottled minced garlic

1/4 teaspoon crushed red pepper

1 (*14 1/2-ounce*) can diced tomatoes

1 (*10-ounce*) package frozen cauliflower, defrosted

1 teaspoon sugar

1/4 teaspoon salt

1/2 teaspoon pepper

1/4 cup crumbled feta cheese

1. In a large skillet over medium heat, heat the olive oil.
   Add the onion, garlic, and crushed red pepper and
   cook until the onions are tender, about 5 minutes.

2. Add the tomatoes, cauliflower, sugar, salt, and pepper,
   stirring well to mix. Simmer for 10 minutes or until
   the cauliflower is cooked to desired tenderness.

3. Transfer to a serving dish, sprinkle with feta cheese
   and toss well to mix.

Cauliflower is a very versatile vegetable and most anything you add to the pan dresses it up nicely. Frozen broccoli florets and baby Brussels sprouts are very nice substitutions in this dish as well.

Couscous Pilaf

SERVINGS: 6
PREPARATION TIME: 5 MINUTES
START TO FINISH TIME: 25 MINUTES

This light side dish lends vibrant color and flavor to any plate. It doubles easily for a crowd, and we have even served it on a brunch buffet to great reviews.

This dish can be prepared ahead, covered, and refrigerated for up to 3 days. To reheat, place the couscous in a microwave-safe serving dish and add a little water to create steam so it does not dry out. Place the dish in a microwave oven and cook on high for 2 minutes, stirring occasionally until heated through. It also freezes well for up to 3 months.

1/4 cup butter or margarine

1 (10-ounce) package frozen peas and carrots

1 (8-ounce) package fresh sliced mushrooms

1 cup frozen chopped onion

1 teaspoon bottled minced garlic

1 (14 1/2-ounce) can chicken broth

1 (10-ounce) box couscous

1/2 teaspoon salt

1/4 teaspoon pepper

1 tablespoon lime juice

1/2 cup slivered almonds

1. In a large saucepan over medium heat, melt the butter or margarine. Add the peas and carrots, mushrooms, onions, and garlic and cook until the vegetables are tender, about 10 minutes.

3. Increase the heat to medium-high. Add the broth and bring to a boil.

4. Add the couscous, salt, and pepper, stirring well to mix. Remove from heat, cover, and let stand for 5 minutes or until the liquid is absorbed.

5. Add the lime juice and almonds, stirring well to mix.

Crisp Cauliflower
and Green Beans

SERVINGS: 10
PREPARATION TIME: 10 MINUTES
START TO FINISH TIME: 20 MINUTES

2 (*10-ounce*) packages frozen cauliflower

1 (*10-ounce*) package frozen cut green beans

4 tablespoons butter or margarine

1 (*2-ounce*) jar diced pimiento, drained

1/2 teaspoon salt

1/4 cup sunflower seed kernels

1. Cook the cauliflower and green beans separately, according to package directions, omitting salt. Drain and set aside.

2. In a large skillet over medium-high heat, melt the butter or margarine. Add the cauliflower and cook, stirring frequently, until the cauliflower is lightly browned and crisp, about 5 minutes.

3. Add the cooked green beans, pimiento, and salt. Cook an additional 2 minutes, until heated through.

4. Transfer to a serving dish and sprinkle with the sunflower seed kernels.

This rich-tasting and colorful dish is perfect holiday fare. It can be made ahead the same day (except for the sunflower seed kernels), covered, and refrigerated. Just before serving, reheat it in a skillet to achieve the crispiness. Transfer to a serving dish and sprinkle with the sunflower seed kernels.

Dijon Cauliflower

This is an elegant way to serve cauliflower. Try substituting grainy mustard for a slightly different flavor and texture.

SERVINGS: 6
PREPARATION TIME: 10 MINUTES
START TO FINISH TIME: 25 MINUTES

2 (*10-ounce*) packages frozen cauliflower, defrosted

3/4 cup grated Parmesan cheese

1/2 cup mayonnaise or salad dressing

1 tablespoon lemon juice

2 tablespoons Dijon-style mustard

1 tablespoon dried parsley

1. Preheat the oven to 375 degrees.

2. Cook cauliflower according to package directions, omitting salt. Drain and set aside.

3. Coat a 2-quart baking dish with cooking spray. Add the cauliflower.

4. In a medium mixing bowl, combine the remaining ingredients, stirring well to mix. Spread the mixture evenly over the cauliflower.

5. Bake for 15 minutes or until lightly browned.

Gingered Beets
with Lemon Yogurt Dressing

SERVINGS: 6
PREPARATION TIME: 5 MINUTES
START TO FINISH TIME: 10 MINUTES

3 tablespoons vegetable oil

1/2 cup frozen chopped onion

1 teaspoon bottled minced garlic

1 teaspoon ground ginger

2 (14-ounce) cans whole or sliced beets,
    drained and rinsed

1 teaspoon salt

1/4 teaspoon pepper

1 (8-ounce) container lemon yogurt

1. In a large skillet over medium heat, heat the
   vegetable oil. Add the onion, garlic, and ginger and
   cook until the onions are tender, about 5 minutes.

2. Add the beets, salt, and pepper, stirring well to mix.

3. Remove from heat and transfer to a large serving bowl
   to cool. Refrigerate until ready to serve.

4. Just before serving, pour the lemon yogurt over the
   beets; toss well to mix.

Robust and radiant beets are accented with an intriguing blend of flavors, sure to please. The beets are best served chilled or at room temperature, so it is a great dish to do ahead. For a nice variation, you can substitute a vinaigrette composed of 1/4 cup lemon juice and 1/4 cup olive oil for the lemon yogurt.

Green Bean Nicoise

We keep many gourmet items stocked in our pantries to make recipes more special when we really want to impress our guests. Substituting one generous tablespoon of tapenade (olive and caper paste) or olivade (olive paste) for the chopped ripe olives, makes this dish more authentic and puts the flavor over the top. Look for these gourmet items near the olives in your market. Don't worry if you cannot find them. This dish tastes great regardless.

SERVINGS: 8
PREPARATION TIME: 5 MINUTES
START TO FINISH TIME: 15 MINUTES

2 (10-ounce) packages frozen whole green beans
1 tablespoon olive oil
1/2 cup frozen chopped onion
1 teaspoon bottled minced garlic
1 (14 1/2-ounce) can diced tomatoes
2 tablespoons chopped ripe olives
2 tablespoons red wine vinegar
2 teaspoons Dijon-style mustard
1/2 teaspoon salt

1. Cook the green beans according to package directions, omitting salt. Drain and set aside in a large serving bowl.

2. In a small skillet over medium heat, heat the olive oil. Add the onion and garlic and cook until the onions are tender, about 5 minutes.

3. Add the remaining ingredients, stirring well to mix. Cook for an additional 2 minutes, or until heated through.

4. Pour the mixture over the green beans; toss well to mix.

Chapter Fifteen — Vegetable Side Dishes

Green Vegetables
with Roasted Red Pepper Puree

SERVINGS: 10
PREPARATION TIME: 10 MINUTES
START TO FINISH TIME: 35 MINUTES

1 (14-ounce) jar roasted red peppers,
    drained well and broken apart with a spoon

1/2 cup frozen chopped onion

1 teaspoon bottled minced garlic

1/4 cup vegetable broth

1 tablespoon red wine vinegar

1 teaspoon lemon juice

1 (10-ounce) package frozen whole green beans

1 (10-ounce) package frozen broccoli florets

1 (10-ounce) package frozen snow peas or sugar snap peas

1/2 teaspoon salt

1. In a small saucepan over medium-high heat, combine all the ingredients except for the green vegetables and salt, stirring well to mix. Bring to a boil, cover, reduce heat to low, and simmer for 20 minutes, stirring occasionally. Remove from heat and let cool.

2. When cooled, transfer the pepper mixture to a food processor or blender container and process or blend until smooth, stopping to scrape down the sides. Return puree to its small saucepan over medium heat and cook 1 minute, stirring constantly until heated through. Pour the red pepper puree onto a large, deep serving platter, distributing evenly.

3. Meanwhile, cook the green vegetables, according to package directions, omitting salt. Drain. Sprinkle with salt; toss well to mix.

4. Arrange the mixed green vegetables on top of the puree. You and your guests can take your vegetables first, and spoon the red pepper puree over the top.

The roasted red peppers create a thick and deeply flavored, fat-free sauce. The green vegetables contrast splendidly with the red sauce, for a very eye-catching presentation. This is a fabulous holiday dish. Frozen asparagus and zucchini are lovely green substitutions. The Roasted Red Pepper Puree can be made up to 3 days ahead and reheated just before serving.

Grilled Portobello Mushrooms

Portobello mushrooms are as versatile as vegetables come. Sliced, they are the perfect companion to any main dish meat or poultry; a fabulous filling for an omelet, frittata, or quesadilla; and topping for pasta or pizza.

Whole portobellos on a toasted bun with choice toppings add up to great vegetarian "burgers" when you are in the mood for something out of the ordinary. We always cook extra and they never go to waste! Try sprinkling them with you favorite dried herbs before serving. We especially like basil, thyme, and tarragon.

SERVINGS: 4
PREPARATION TIME: 10 MINUTES
START TO FINISH TIME: 20 MINUTES,
                      PLUS MARINATING TIME

4 medium to large portobello mushrooms

1/4 cup olive oil

1 tablespoon balsamic vinegar

1 tablespoon bottled minced garlic

1/2 teaspoon salt or soy sauce or tamari

1/4 teaspoon pepper

1. Rinse the mushrooms quickly under running water. Remove the stems and discard or reserve for another use.

2. In a large resealable plastic bag, combine the remaining ingredients, shaking well to mix.

3. Add the mushrooms; turn to coat with the marinade. Refrigerate for 1 hour, turning the bag occasionally.

4. When ready to cook, prepare the grill to medium heat. Place the mushrooms, top side up, directly on the grill or in a grill basket. Cook the mushrooms for 5 minutes on each side, or until lightly charred on the outside and tender on the inside.

Mushroom Barley Casserole

SERVINGS: 8
PREPARATION TIME: 15 MINUTES
START TO FINISH TIME: 45 MINUTES

1 stick butter or margarine

1 (*10-ounce*) package frozen chopped onions

1 (*16-ounce*) package fresh sliced mushrooms

1-1/2 cups quick-cooking pearl barley

1/2 cup pine nuts

1 (*14 1/2-ounce*) can chicken broth

1/2 teaspoon salt

1/4 teaspoon pepper

1. Preheat the oven to 350 degrees.

2. In a large ovenproof skillet over medium heat, melt the butter or margarine. Add the onions and cook until tender, about 5 minutes.

3. Add the mushrooms and cook another 5 minutes.

4. Add the barley and pine nuts; cook, stirring constantly, 1 minute.

5. Add the broth, salt, and pepper, stirring well to mix. Increase the heat to medium-high, and bring to a boil. Remove from heat; cover.

6. Transfer the skillet to the oven and bake for 30 minutes or until liquid is absorbed.

When rice and pasta seem too mundane, barley is a delightfully textured grain to rejuvenate your main course. If you don't have an ovenproof skillet, just transfer the mixture to a 2-quart casserole dish that has been coated with cooking spray.

Orange Glazed Carrots

SERVINGS: 4
PREPARATION TIME: 5 MINUTES
START TO FINISH TIME: 20 MINUTES

1/2 cup water

1 (*16-ounce*) package fresh baby carrots

1/3 cup orange marmalade

1/2 cup golden raisins

1/4 cup slivered almonds

1. In a medium saucepan, bring the water to a boil.

2. Add the carrots; return to a boil. Reduce heat to medium; cover and cook the carrots 10 to 12 minutes or desired tenderness, stirring occasionally. Drain and return to saucepan.

3. Add marmalade and raisins, stirring well to mix.

4. Cook over low heat for 1 minute or until marmalade is melted, stirring constantly.

5. Add almonds; toss gently to mix.

Rice with Dried Fruit and Nuts

SERVINGS: 8
PREPARATION TIME: 10 MINUTES
START TO FINISH TIME: 30 MINUTES

1/2 stick butter or margarine

1 cup frozen chopped onion

1 (*32-ounce*) container chicken broth

2 cups basmati rice

1/2 cup dried cranberries, raisins, or mixed fruit bits

1 teaspoon salt

1/2 cup sliced almonds

1. In a large saucepan over medium-high heat, melt the butter or margarine. Add the onions and cook until tender, about 5 minutes.

2. Add the chicken broth, rice, dried fruit, and salt. Bring to a boil, cover, reduce the heat to medium-low, and simmer for 20 minutes, or until all the liquid is absorbed.

3. Add almonds, stirring well to mix.

We love the smell of Basmati rice as it cooks. It fills your home with the aroma of popping corn. If you are unable to find Basmati rice, substitute your favorite rice. Look for a variety of dried fruits in your supermarket next to the raisins. Cashews and pistachios offer a unique alternative for the almonds. Have fun experimenting with different rices, fruits, and nuts, and this dish will never become boring. It freezes well for up to 3 months.

Sautéed Spinach
and White Beans

SERVINGS: 8
PREPARATION TIME: 5 MINUTES
START TO FINISH TIME: 20 MINUTES

2 tablespoons olive oil

1 cup frozen chopped onion

1 tablespoon bottled minced garlic

2 (*15- to 19-ounce*) cans cannellini beans,
  rinsed and drained

2 tablespoons white wine vinegar

2 (*10-ounce*) packages fresh washed baby spinach

1/2 teaspoon thyme

1 teaspoon salt

1/4 teaspoon pepper

1. In a large skillet over medium heat, heat the olive
   oil. Add onion and garlic and cook until the onions
   are tender, about 5 minutes.

2. Add the beans, and cook until heated through and
   slightly softened, about 3 minutes.

3. Add the vinegar and spinach (*in batches if necessary*),
   and cook for 3 minutes, stirring frequently
   until wilted.

4. Add the thyme, salt, and pepper, stirring well to mix.

This dish can pull double-duty as a side dish for dinner, then a light lunch the next day. White wine vinegar adds tangy flavor to the spinach. Red wine vinegar or sherry vinegar can be substituted for a slightly different and pleasant variation.

Cooking a large amount of spinach is easy—just sauté it in batches. As it wilts, it creates room in your pan.

Chapter Fifteen — Vegetable Side Dishes

Snacking Corn Bread

SERVINGS: 8
PREPARATION TIME: 10 MINUTES
START TO FINISH TIME: 45 MINUTES

2 large eggs

1/2 cup vegetable oil

1 (8-ounce) container sour cream

1 (7-ounce) can creamed corn

1 cup cornmeal mix

1. Preheat the oven to 375 degrees.

2. Coat an 8-inch square pan with cooking spray.

3. In a large mixing bowl, combine the eggs, oil,
   sour cream, and corn, stirring well to mix.
   Add the cornmeal and stir until thoroughly mixed.

4. Pour batter into the prepared pan and bake for
   35 minutes or until lightly browned around the edges.

This recipe comes from Nathalie Dupree. When Cynthia produced Nathalie's first television series, "New Southern Cooking," this recipe enchanted her. It was perhaps the ease of preparation and the fact that Cynthia was a new cook. She would add a warm bowl of soup for a very satisfying meal. Cornmeal mix is corn meal with salt and leavening already mixed in—a nice shortcut for the cook. A heavy baking pan versus a glass baking dish ensures the required crustiness.

Spinach and Onion Couscous

This dish is a delicious and colorful companion to most any main meal.

SERVINGS: 4
PREPARATION TIME: 5 MINUTES
START TO FINISH TIME: 25 MINUTES

2 tablespoons olive oil

1 cup frozen chopped onion

1 teaspoon bottled minced garlic

1 (*14 1/2-ounce*) can chicken broth

1 (*10-ounce*) package frozen chopped spinach

1 (*10-ounce*) box couscous

3/4 cup grated Parmesan cheese

2 tablespoons lemon juice

1/2 teaspoon salt

1/4 teaspoon pepper

1/2 cup chopped pecans

1. In a large saucepan over medium-high heat, heat the olive oil. Add the onions and the garlic and cook until the onions are tender, about 5 minutes.

2. Add the broth and spinach; cook, stirring occasionally, until spinach thaws. Bring to a boil.

3. Add the couscous, stirring well to mix. Remove from heat, cover, and let stand 5 minutes, or until liquid is absorbed.

4. Add remaining ingredients, stirring well to mix.

Chapter Fifteen — Vegetable Side Dishes

Spinach with Lemon and Pepper

SERVINGS: 2
PREPARATION TIME: 5 MINUTES
START TO FINISH TIME: 10 MINUTES

1 teaspoon olive oil

1 teaspoon dark sesame oil

1 teaspoon soy sauce or tamari

1/8 teaspoon crushed red pepper

1 (*10-ounce*) package fresh washed baby spinach

1 tablespoon lemon juice

1. In a large skillet over medium-high heat, heat the olive oil, sesame oil, soy sauce or tamari, and crushed red pepper until hot but not smoking, about 1 minute.

2. Add the spinach and cook for 3 to 4 minutes, stirring frequently until wilted.

3. Transfer to a serving dish. Drizzle the lemon juice over the spinach.

The great variety of flavors in this dish work very well with the spinach.

Sugar Snap Peas with Cashews

SERVINGS: 4
PREPARATION TIME: 5 MINUTES
START TO FINISH TIME: 10 MINUTES

1 (*16-ounce*) package frozen sugar snap peas

1/3 cup orange juice

1 tablespoon honey

1 teaspoon cornstarch

1/4 teaspoon dried orange peel

1/4 cup cashews

1. Cook sugar snap peas according to package directions, omitting salt. Drain and set aside in a serving dish.

2. In a small saucepan over medium-high heat, combine the orange juice, honey, and cornstarch, stirring well to mix. Stir constantly for 2 to 3 minutes until thickened.

3. Add orange peel and cashews, stirring well to mix.

4. Pour sauce over the peas; toss well to coat.

Sugar snap peas are naturally sweet and tender with plump edible pods. The delicate sauce here compliments them nicely, while cashews add a delightful crunch. You can substitute snow peas, a close relative, with similar results.

Thai Rice

SERVINGS: 8
PREPARATION TIME: 10 MINUTES
START TO FINISH TIME: 20 MINUTES

1 stick butter or margarine

1 (*10-ounce*) package frozen chopped onion

1 teaspoon salt

1 teaspoon ground ginger

2 teaspoons curry powder

6 cups cooked long-grain white rice (*2 cups dry rice*)

1 (*3 1/2-ounce*) can sweetened shredded coconut
  (*about 1 cup*)

1 cup peach or mango chutney

1. In a small skillet over medium-high heat, melt the butter or margarine. Add the onion and cook until tender, about 5 minutes

2. Add the salt, ginger, and curry, stirring well to mix, and cook until fragrant, about 1 minute. Remove from heat and set aside.

3. In a large mixing bowl, combine the remaining ingredients, stirring well to mix.

4. Add the onion mixture, stirring well to mix.

This aromatic rice is teeming with flavor and is the perfect companion for our **Grilled Thai Chicken Thighs**. *The two dishes in combination make for an easy weekend barbecue with friends. The rice can be prepared ahead, covered, and refrigerated for up to 3 days. To reheat, place the rice in a serving dish and add a little water to create steam so the rice does not dry out. Place the dish in a microwave oven and cook on high for 2 minutes, stirring occasionally until the rice is heated through.*

This recipe can be made in advance and is very "tote-able".

Wild Rice
with Green Beans, Spinach, and Oranges

SERVINGS: 6
PREPARATION TIME: 20 MINUTES
START TO FINISH TIME: 30 MINUTES

1 (6-ounce) package long-grain and wild rice mix

1 (10-ounce) box frozen, cut green beans

1 tablespoon olive oil

1 (10-ounce) package fresh washed baby spinach

1 (15-ounce) can Mandarin oranges, drained

1/2 cup bottled Italian dressing

1/2 teaspoon salt

1/4 teaspoon pepper

1. Cook the rice according to package directions; cool.

2. Cook the green beans according to package directions, omitting salt. Drain and set aside to cool.

3. Meanwhile, in a large skillet over medium-high heat, heat the olive oil. Add the spinach and cook for 3 minutes, stirring frequently until wilted; cool.

4. In a large serving bowl, combine the cooled cooked rice, green beans, and spinach with the remaining ingredients. Toss well to mix. Serve at room temperature, or chill and serve cold.

Winter Squash
with Butter and Maple Syrup

SERVINGS: 6
PREPARATION TIME: 10 MINUTES
START TO FINISH TIME: 20 MINUTES

2 (*10-ounce*) packages frozen winter squash

1/2 teaspoon salt

1/4 teaspoon pepper

1/2 stick butter or margarine

1/4 cup maple-flavored syrup

1. Cook squash according to package directions, omitting salt. Set aside.

2. In a small saucepan over medium heat, melt the butter or margarine. Reduce heat to low and add maple-flavored syrup, stirring well to mix.

3. In a medium mixing bowl, combine squash, salt, pepper, and half of the butter-maple syrup mixture, stirring well to mix. Transfer to a serving dish.

4. Pour rest of butter-maple syrup mixture over the top.

Maple syrup gives this squash an upscale, yet homey flavor. Feel free to make this dish early in the day or even the day before serving.

Desserts

Catherine has developed a bit of a reputation among her children's friends, one about which she is surprisingly flattered. They call her *"the cookie mom,"* because she is constantly baking.

Whatever the time of day or occasion, nothing rivals the flavor and feeling one gets from homemade cookies, warm out of the oven. While having babies and holding babies presented certain challenges, they never stopped Catherine from baking, they merely slowed her down. From time to time she has contemplated baking for profit. But for now, she bakes for carpool, for little league, for friends, for holiday gifts, for potlucks, and always for fun.

Baking is so much more than just following a recipe. It is math, chemistry, and art all sifted, mixed, and rolled into one. Like poetry or music, it is also a great way to express oneself, whether it's fun and fruity like a flaky apple strudel or sexy and hedonistic like a chocolate hazelnut torte. **Nothing marks a special occasion or completes a fine meal better than something sweet.** Dessert has even become an expectation at most gatherings. However, it may be the most difficult course to pull off while holding a baby.

You have probably already sampled the vast variety of prepared baked goods available in your local supermarket or corner bakery and know that they are reasonable, if not preferable, alternatives to homemade. So why forgo the convenience for all the fuss? Homemade desserts communicate a message that you care enough to take the time to make it yourself. Your family and friends will be so impressed when you make it from scratch, plus...you get to lick the spoon!

The recipes that we have chosen make the formidable friendly and the elegant easy. With a little bit of planning, all of them can be made hours to days ahead, and many can be frozen. **With a well-stocked pantry and no notice at all, several of our desserts can be quickly prepared on the spot and served fresh to the amazement of your unexpected guests.**

There are classics along with new favorites which are certain to satisfy even the most discerning sweet tooth. Cynthia always relies on the **Peach Cobbler** recipe when she must entertain unexpectedly. Peaches are a staple in her freezer and the other ingredients are always stocked in her pantry. This bubbling, hot dessert pulled fresh from her oven never fails to comfort and impress her guests.

Always buy the finest quality ingredients at your disposal; we truly believe they impact the quality of the finished product. If you do not bake often enough, store your staples (*flour, sugar, brown sugar, nuts, chocolate bars, chips, and cocoa powder*) in airtight containers in the refrigerator to ensure freshness.

Unless whole-wheat flour is specifically called for, use only unbleached and unbromated all-purpose white flour. Pure vanilla extract adds a richer flavor to batters and sauces than artificial vanilla flavoring. Use the finest quality chocolate you can find to make more decadent chocolate desserts. We always prefer butter to margarine, but you can choose for yourself.

No one should ever know how virtually effortless these desserts are. Just accept their praise graciously, and let them be duly impressed.

Apple Crisp

We made this traditional favorite quick and easy by using tasty, frozen escalloped apples. This shortcut eliminates the nearly impossible (for one- armed cooks) task of peeling and slicing fresh apples and cuts the cooking time in half.

SERVINGS: 6
PREPARATION TIME: 10 MINUTES .
START TO FINISH TIME: 35 MINUTES

2 (*12-ounce*) packages frozen escalloped apples, defrosted

1/2 cup light brown sugar, firmly packed

1/4 cup all-purpose flour

1/4 cup chopped pecans

1/4 teaspoon ground cinnamon

1/8 teaspoon ground nutmeg

1/2 stick butter or margarine, melted

vanilla ice cream, optional

1. Preheat the oven to 350 degrees.

2. Coat a 9-inch pie plate with cooking spray.

3. Place the apples into the prepared pie plate.

4. In a small mixing bowl, combine brown sugar, flour, pecans, cinnamon, and nutmeg, stirring well to mix; sprinkle evenly over the apples.

5. Pour the melted butter or margarine evenly over the sugar mixture.

6. Bake for 25 minutes until apples are bubbling and the top is lightly browned.

7. Serve warm with vanilla ice cream, if desired.

Baby's 1st Birthday Cake

SERVINGS: 9
PREPARATION TIME: 15 MINUTES
START TO FINISH TIME: 45 MINUTES

1 cup apple juice concentrate

1 cup raisins, divided

1/2 cup dates

1/2 stick butter or margarine

1-1/2 teaspoons ground cinnamon

3/4 cup whole-wheat flour

1/2 cup wheat germ

1 tablespoon baking powder

1. Preheat the oven to 325 degrees.

2. Coat an 8-inch square baking pan with cooking spray. Set aside.

3. Place the apple juice concentrate, 1/2 cup of the raisins, and the dates in a food processor or blender container and process or blend until smooth, stopping to scrape down the sides.

4. In a small saucepan over medium heat, melt the butter or margarine. Add the fruit mixture, the remaining raisins, and cinnamon, stirring well to mix. Set aside to cool slightly.

5. In a medium mixing bowl, combine the flour, wheat germ, and baking powder, stirring well to mix. Add the contents of the saucepan, stirring until just mixed. Do not overmix.

6. Pour the batter into the prepared baking pan. Bake for 25 minutes, or until a toothpick inserted into the center comes out clean. Cover loosely with foil during baking if the cake starts to brown.

Although the scrapbook pictures will not be quite as dramatic with frosting smeared from head to toe, this cake, adapted from **What to Expect the First Year**, is a perfect choice for baby's first birthday, especially if your pediatrician has not given the go-ahead for eggs or dairy products. It's also a yummy snack or dessert that can be enjoyed year-round by a health-conscious family.

It makes one single-layer 8-inch square cake. To keep the cake from becoming too dry and crumbly for baby to gum, store in a resealable plastic bag as soon as it has cooled.

Banana Cake

*Catherine always makes homemade banana cake, a cherished tradition from her childhood, for her own children on the occasion of their birthdays (one layer for each year—the cakes are getting pretty tall!). When it is her birthday (too many layers to count), Catherine's husband and her three children collaborate to make this cake especially for her. They all love this wonderful adaptation from **The Silver Palate Cookbook.***

SERVINGS: 12
PREPARATION TIME: 20 MINUTES
START TO FINISH TIME: 1 HOUR

2 sticks butter or margarine (*please use butter!*), softened to room temperature

1 cup sugar

2 large eggs

1 cup mashed ripe banana

1-3/4 cups flour

1/2 teaspoon salt

1 teaspoon baking soda

1/4 cup milk

1 teaspoon vanilla

Cream Cheese Frosting

1. Preheat the oven to 350 degrees.

2. Coat two 9-inch layer cake pans with cooking spray.

3. In a large mixing bowl or in the bowl of a standing mixer, combine butter or margarine and sugar. Mix on high for 1 minute, until light and fluffy.

3. Add eggs, one at a time, beating well after each addition.

4. Add mashed banana, and beat for 1 minute.

5. In a medium mixing bowl, combine the flour, salt, and baking soda, stirring well to mix. Add to banana mixture. On low speed, continue mixing until thoroughly mixed.

6. Add milk and vanilla. Mix for 1 minute.

7. Pour batter into the prepared pans. Bake for 25 to 30 minutes or until a toothpick inserted into the center comes out clean.

8. Cool in pans on a rack for 10 minutes. Unmold and cool on rack for 2 hours.

9. When cooled, place one layer on a serving plate and frost with **Cream Cheese Frosting**; cover with second layer and frost top and sides of cake.

Blender Chocolate Soufflé

SERVINGS: 6
PREPARATION TIME: 10 MINUTES
START TO FINISH TIME: 1 HOUR, 10 MINUTES

Your guests will think you labored for hours over this impressive dessert, that is actually very easy on the chef. The batter can be made several hours ahead and refrigerated in the prepared soufflé dish. Take the dish out of the refrigerator 3 hours before you plan to serve it. Allow it to sit at room temperature for 2 hours, then bake it for one hour at 375 degrees.
For individual soufflés, you can pour equal amounts of the batter into six ramekins that have been coated with cooking spray.
Place them together on a baking sheet and reduce the baking time to 40 minutes.
If you don't have a blender, get one! A blender is almost indispensable.
A soufflé dish is simply a 1-quart round baking dish.

1 cup heavy cream

1 (*12-ounce*) package semisweet chocolate chips

1 (*8-ounce*) package cream cheese, room temperature, cut in 4 pieces

5 large eggs

2 teaspoons vanilla

whipped cream or vanilla ice cream, optional

1. Preheat the oven to 375 degrees.

2. Coat a 1 1/2-quart soufflé dish with cooking spray.

3. In a large glass measuring cup, microwave cream on high for 1-1/2 to 2 minutes, until boiling.

4. Pour boiling cream into a blender container. Add the chocolate chips and blend for 1 minute until all the chocolate is melted and smooth.

5. With the blender running at lowest speed, add cream cheese (*one piece at a time*), eggs (*one at a time*), and vanilla, and continue blending for 15 seconds until well mixed. Pour batter into prepared soufflé dish.

6. Bake for 1 hour. Soufflé puffs delicately above the top of the dish.

7. With the back of a serving spoon, break an opening in the center of the hot soufflé and fill with whipped cream or vanilla ice cream, if desired.

Chapter Sixteen — Desserts

Blender Coconut Pie

SERVINGS: 8
PREPARATION TIME: 10 MINUTES
START TO FINISH TIME: 55 MINUTES

4 large eggs

2 cups milk

1/4 cup butter or margarine, melted

2 teaspoons vanilla

3/4 cup sugar

1/2 cup all-purpose flour

1 teaspoon baking powder

1 (*3 1/2-ounce*) can sweetened shredded coconut

1. Preheat the oven to 350 degrees.

2. Coat a 9-inch glass pie dish with cooking spray.

3. Place all the ingredients except for the coconut in a blender container, and blend for 1 minute, until well mixed. Pour this mixture into the prepared pie dish. Sprinkle with the coconut.

4. Bake for 45 minutes, or until the center is set and the top is toasted golden brown.

5. Let cool on a wire rack for 30 minutes before serving.

Yes, you really can make a pie in a blender! Simple and delicious, this pie even makes its own crust. Homemade desserts do not get any easier! Refrigerate any leftovers.

Blender Pecan Pie

SERVINGS: 8
PREPARATION TIME: 10 MINUTES
START TO FINISH TIME: 45 MINUTES

Catherine was not born in the South, but she spent 14 years in Atlanta (where she left her heart) and can still make a pretty mean pecan pie. Here is a fine Southern tradition made easy.

Do not rinse your measuring cup after you add the cream to the blender container. The cream leaves a nice coating in the cup, which helps the corn syrup glide out without sticking.

Refrigerate any leftovers, but be sure to reheat before serving again. The pie can be frozen for up to 3 months.

3 large eggs

1/2 cup heavy cream

1/2 cup light corn syrup

2 tablespoons butter or margarine, melted

1 cup dark brown sugar

1 teaspoon vanilla

1/8 teaspoon salt

2 cups chopped pecans

1 (9-inch) frozen pie crust, unbaked

1. Preheat the oven to 400 degrees.

2. Place eggs, cream, corn syrup, butter, brown sugar, vanilla, and salt in a blender container and blend for 10 seconds or until well mixed.

3. Sprinkle chopped pecans in the pie crust. Pour blended mixture over pecans.

4. Bake for 30 to 35 minutes, or until the filling is set and golden brown on top.

5. Let cool on a wire rack for 30 minutes before serving.

Cherry or Blueberry Pie

SERVINGS: 8
PREPARATION TIME: 10 MINUTES
START TO FINISH TIME: 1 HOUR, 10 MINUTES

3 (*12-ounce*) packages frozen dark sweet cherries or
   frozen blueberries, partially thawed

3 tablespoons cornstarch

1/4 cup, plus 1 tablespoon sugar

1 (*15-ounce*) package refrigerated pie crusts

1. Preheat the oven to 400 degrees.

2. In a large mixing bowl, combine the cherries,
   cornstarch, and 1/4 cup sugar, stirring well to mix.
   Set aside.

2. Unfold one pie crust and place in a 9-inch pie plate.
   Add the cherry mixture, then brush the rim of the pie
   crust with water. This seals the crusts together.

3. Unfold the second pie crust over the top of the pie.
   Run a knife around the edge of the pie plate to cut off
   the excess dough and make the edge of the crust flush
   with the pie plate.With the tines of a fork, press down
   around the top rim edge of the pie - this makes for a
   nice decorative edge as well as sealing the
   crusts together.

4. Sprinkle the top with the remaining sugar. Cut four
   small slits in the top crust for air vents.

5. Place the pie plate on a cookie sheet in the oven and
   bake for 20 minutes.

6. Lower the oven temperature to 350 degrees and
   continue baking the pie for another 40 minutes.
   Let cool on a wire rack before serving.

Ever since Cynthia discovered refrigerated pie crusts, pies have become her favorite dessert to make for company. It is so easy to pop a pie in the oven, and her guests are always impressed with the results. Cynthia makes them early in the day and serves them at room temperature after dinner. Refrigerate any leftovers. Try cherry or blueberry, or a mixture of both!

Chocolate Nut Pie

SERVINGS: 8
PREPARATION TIME: 10 MINUTES
START TO FINISH TIME: 1 HOUR

1 (6-ounce) package semisweet chocolate chips

2 cups chopped macadamia nuts, pecans, or walnuts

1 (9-inch) frozen pie crust, unbaked

3 large eggs, lightly beaten

1 cup light corn syrup

1 cup sugar

2 tablespoons butter or margarine, melted

1 teaspoon vanilla

whipped cream, optional

1. Preheat the oven to 350 degrees.

2. Place the chocolate chips and nuts in the bottom of the pie crust.

3. In a large mixing bowl using a wire whisk, combine the eggs, corn syrup, sugar, butter or margarine, and vanilla, stirring well to mix. Pour the mixture over the chocolate chips and nuts.

4. Bake for 45 to 50 minutes, or until the filling is set and golden brown on top.

5. Let cool on a wire rack for 30 minutes before serving.

6. Serve with whipped cream, if desired.

*Catherine helped to prepare this recipe of Nathalie Dupree's for Julia Child and Burt Wolf on the PBS special, **An American Feast**. The original recipe is very easy to assemble, but we've made it even easier for the one-armed cook.*

The pie may be made several days ahead, or frozen for up to 3 months. If you coat your measuring cup with cooking spray, the corn syrup glides out without sticking.

Cream Cheese Frosting

YIELD: ABOUT 2 CUPS
PREPARATION TIME: 10 MINUTES
START TO FINISH TIME: 10 MINUTES

1 (8-ounce) package cream cheese, at room temperature

1 stick butter or margarine, at room temperature

1 (1-pound) box confectioner's sugar

1 teaspoon vanilla

1. In a large mixing bowl or in the bowl of a standing mixer, combine cream cheese and butter. Mix on high speed for 1 minute, until light and fluffy.

2. Add confectioner's sugar and vanilla. On low speed, continue mixing for 2 minutes, until light and fluffy and thoroughly mixed. Mixture should be free of lumps.

3. Frost **Banana Cake** or any cake. This frosting is delicious!

This recipe, adapted from **The Silver Palate Cookbook**, *frosts a 2-layer* **Banana Cake**. *How sweet it is!*

Frozen Lemonade Pie

This is a light and refreshing dessert that brings memories of our summers in Maine. The ingredients are easy to come by and are easy to assemble. Make this pie at your favorite home away from home on your summer vacation. Limeade may be substituted for the lemonade to make an easy Frozen Key Lime Pie.

SERVINGS: 8
PREPARATION TIME: 10 MINUTES
START TO FINISH TIME: 10 MINUTES,
                  PLUS 3 HOURS FOR FREEZING

1 (6-ounce) can frozen lemonade concentrate

1 (14-ounce) can sweetened condensed milk

1 (12-ounce) container frozen nondairy whipped
   topping, thawed

1 (9-inch) prepared graham cracker crust

1. In a large mixing bowl, combine the lemonade and sweetened condensed milk, stirring well to mix with a wire whisk until smooth.

2. Add the nondairy whipped topping, stirring well to mix.

3. Pour, or scoop, the filling into the graham cracker crust.

4. Cover with the prepared graham cracker crust plastic cover, seal, and freeze for at least 3 hours or overnight.

Layered Cookie Bars

SERVINGS: 24
PREPARATION TIME: 10 MINUTES
START TO FINISH TIME: 40 MINUTES

1 stick butter or margarine, melted

2 cups graham cracker crumbs

1 (*14-ounce*) can sweetened condensed milk

1 cup sweetened shredded coconut

1 (*12-ounce*) package semisweet chocolate chips

1 cup chopped walnuts or pecans

1. Preheat the oven to 350 degrees.

2. In a 9 x 13-inch glass baking dish, melt the butter or margarine in the microwave.

3. Sprinkle the graham cracker crumbs evenly over the melted butter or margarine.

4. Pour the sweetened condensed milk evenly over the crumbs.

5. Sprinkle the shredded coconut, chocolate chips and walnuts or pecans evenly over the sweetened condensed milk layer; press down gently with your hand or the back of a rubber spatula.

6. Bake for 25 to 30 minutes or until lightly browned.

7. Let cool in the pan on a wire rack for 30 minutes. Cut into 24 bars.

This is our favorite "dump" recipe—dump all the ingredients into a dish, bake, and out comes something truly spectacular.

Keep all the ingredients on hand, and you can have warm cookie bars in minutes when guests drop by unexpectedly, or make an extra batch for the freezer, cut into bars, and freeze for up to 3 months.

Peach Cobbler

Peach Cobbler has become somewhat of a "signature" dessert at Cynthia's house. It is nearly effortless to mix together, and if you pop this dessert in the oven before you sit down to dinner, it will be ready to serve when dinner is finished.

This recipe comes from Cynthia's dear friend, Nathalie Dupree, who has taught her much about comfortable entertaining.

Substitute the peaches with any frozen fruit (like cherries or blueberries), and when you have two hands available, fresh fruit is wonderful, too.

SERVINGS: 6
PREPARATION TIME: 5 MINUTES
START TO FINISH TIME: 35 MINUTES

1 stick butter or margarine

1 cup all-purpose flour

1-1/2 teaspoons baking powder

1/2 teaspoon salt

1 cup milk

1/2 cup sugar

1 (16-ounce) package frozen peach slices

1. Preheat the oven to 350 degrees.

2. In a 9 x 13-inch glass baking dish, melt the butter or margarine in the microwave.

3. In a large mixing bowl, combine the flour, baking powder, salt, milk, and sugar, stirring well to mix with a wire whisk.

4. Pour the batter evenly over the hot melted butter or margarine.

5. Top batter evenly with the peach slices.

6. Bake for 45 minutes. The batter will puff around the fruit and become slightly browned.

Pineapple Cake

SERVINGS: 18
PREPARATION TIME: 10 MINUTES
START TO FINISH TIME: 45 MINUTES

2 cups all-purpose flour

1-1/2 cups sugar

2 teaspoons baking soda

1/2 teaspoon salt

1 (20-ounce) can crushed pineapple, in unsweetened juice

2 large eggs

whipped cream, optional

1. Preheat the oven to 350 degrees.

2. Coat a 9 x 13-inch glass baking dish with
   cooking spray.

3. In a large mixing bowl, combine all of the ingredients
   except for the whipped cream, stirring well to mix.

4. Pour batter into prepared dish and bake for
   30 to 35 minutes.

5. Allow to cool slightly before cutting.

6. Top with whipped cream, if desired.

This cake is a favorite of Cynthia's son's dear friend, Eliot, who is allergic to dairy products. She serves it warm with a mound of nondairy whipped topping, and it never fails to please. Any leftovers keep well for several days in the refrigerator for handy snacking.

The Perfect Brownie

SERVINGS: 16
PREPARATION TIME: 10 MINUTES
START TO FINISH TIME: 40 MINUTES

1-1/2 sticks butter or margarine

1 cup finest quality unsweetened cocoa powder

1-3/4 cups dark brown sugar

pinch salt

2 teaspoons vanilla

3 large eggs

1 cup all-purpose flour

1. Preheat the oven to 375 degrees.

2. Coat an 8-inch square baking dish with cooking spray.

3. In a large saucepan over medium heat, melt the butter or margarine. Remove from heat.

4. Add the cocoa powder, brown sugar, salt, vanilla, and eggs, stirring well until mixed and smooth.

5. Add the flour, stirring well to mix.

6. Pour the batter into the prepared baking dish. Bake for 30 minutes, until the top is dry but the center looks moist. Do not overbake.

7. Let cool in the dish on a wire rack for at least 30 minutes, or until firm. Cut into 16 squares.

We have experimented with many brownie recipes over the years in pursuit of perfection and believe we have found it! Hopefully other chocolate connoisseurs will appreciate their deep color; seductively rich, chocolate nose; beautifully intense, succulent flavor; lush voluptuous texture; soft, lip-smacking finish. The Perfect Brownie.

White Chocolate Blondies
with Macadamia Nuts

SERVINGS: 16
PREPARATION TIME: 10 MINUTES
START TO FINISH TIME: 45 MINUTES

1 stick butter or margarine

1-1/4 cups brown sugar, firmly packed

1 teaspoon vanilla

2 large eggs

1 cup all-purpose flour

1 (3 1/4-ounce) jar macadamia nuts

1 cup white chocolate chips

1. Preheat the oven to 350 degrees.

2. Coat an 8-inch square baking dish with cooking spray.

3. In a large mixing bowl or in the bowl of a standing mixer, combine the butter or margarine, brown sugar, and vanilla. Mix on high for 1 minute, until light and fluffy.

4. Add the eggs, mixing on low until fully incorporated; then increase the speed to high and continue mixing for 2 minutes, until light and fluffy.

5. Reduce the speed to low, add the flour, and continue mixing until fully incorporated.

6. Fold in the nuts and chocolate with a spoon, until just blended.

7. Spread the batter in the prepared pan and bake for 35 minutes, or until a toothpick inserted in the center comes out clean.

8. Let cool in the pan on a wire rack for at least 30 minutes. Cut into 16 squares.

These cookies are well worth the hassle of getting out the mixer. You won't be sorry! You can substitute semisweet chocolate chips or milk chocolate chips for a nice variation. When we really want to go all out, we substitute 2 (3 1/2-ounce) gourmet white chocolate candy bars, broken into coarse chunks for the chips.

The finished cookie squares can be stored in an airtight container at room temperature for 3 days, if they last that long!

Menus

Weekend Barbecue I
Serves 4
Mushroom Soup
    (omit rice)
Wine Marinated Rosemary Rib Eyes
Wild Rice with Green Beans,
    Spinach, and Oranges
Herb Cheese Bread
Apple Crisp

Weekend Barbecue II
Serves 4
Cheesy Artichoke Bites
Grilled Tilapia
    with Cilantro-Orange Dressing
Rice with Dried Fruit and Nuts
Cauliflower with Tomatoes and Feta
Frozen Lemonade Pie

Weekend Barbecue III
Serves 8
Grilled Thai Chicken Thighs
Thai Rice
Broccoli Slaw Salad
Pineapple Cake

Romantic Dinner I
Serves 2
Tomato and Yogurt Soup
Sautéed Veal Cutlets
    with Goat Cheese,
    Wild Mushrooms, and Spinach
Crusty Bread
The Perfect Brownie

Romantic Dinner II
Serves 2
Shrimp Soup with Tomatoes and Feta
Rack of Lamb for 2
Spinach with Lemon and Pepper
Tossed Green Salad
Crusty Bread
Cherry Pie

Mexican-Inspired Dinner
Serves 4
Creative Quesadillas
Vegetarian Chili
Snacking Corn Bread
Tossed Green Salad
Frozen Lemonade Pie

Tuscan-Inspired Dinner
Serves 8
White Bean Dip
Chickpea and Red Pepper Dip
Olives
Pasta Putanesca *(doubled)*
Garlic Parmesean Spread (for GCB's)
Tossed Green Salad
The Perfect Brownie
Ice Cream

Fall Dinner Party
  Serves 6-8
Curried Squash Soup
Beef Tenderloin
Mushroom Barley Casserole
Green Vegetables
    with Roasted Red Pepper Puree
Blender Chocolate Soufflé

Menus

Fall Dinner I
Serves 4
Broccoli Cheddar Soup
Brisket
Orange Glazed Carrots
Spinach and Onion Couscous
Peach Cobbler

Fall Dinner II
Serves 6
Mushroom Soup
Tomato Cream Shrimp in Pastry Shells
Green Bean Nicoise
Peach Cobbler

Winter Dinner Party
Serves 8
Curried Carrot Spread
White Bean Dip
Beef Tenderloin
Wild Rice with Green Beans,
    Spinach, and Oranges
Cottage Dill and Onion Bread
Chocolate Nut Pie

Winter Dinner I
Serves 4
Mushroom Soup
    (*use wild mushrooms*)
Steaks with White Beans and Spinach
Orange Glazed Carrots
Crusty Bread
Peach Cobbler

Winter Dinner II
Serves 6
Pork Chops with Blackberry Preserves
Dijon Cauliflower
Spinach and Onion Couscous (*doubled*)
Pineapple Cake

Spring Dinner Party
Serves 6-8
Cheesy Artichoke Bites
Roast Leg of Lamb
Rice with Dried Fruit and Nuts
Green Vegetables
    with Roasted Red Pepper Puree
Blender Pecan Pie

Spring Dinner I
Serves 4
Ginger-Sherry Lamb Chops
Spinach and Onion Couscous
Gingered Beets
    with Lemon Yogurt Dressing
Blender Chocolate Soufflé

Spring Dinner II
Serves 8
My Chicken Thighs
Broccoli Slaw Salad
Herb Cheese Bread
White Chocolate Blondies
    with Macadamia Nuts

Summer Dinner Party
Serves 8
Curried Carrot Spread
Spicy Broccoli Spread
White Bean Dip
Mediterranean Chicken
Plain Steamed Rice
Tossed Green Salad
Chocolate Nut Pie

Menus

Summer Dinner I
Serves 4
Black Bean Soup
Caribbean Shrimp
Plain Couscous or Plain Rice
Tossed Green Salad
Blender Coconut Pie

Summer Dinner II
Serves 4
Fish with Tarragon Tomato Sauce
Broccoli with Water Chestnuts
Plain Rice
Frozen Lemonade Pie
  (key lime variation)

Holiday Meal I
Serves 6-8
Curried Squash Soup
Holiday Roast with Madeira Sauce
Mushroom Barley Casserole
Crisp Cauliflower and Green Beans
Blender Coconut Pie

Holiday Meal II
Serves 8-10
Curried Squash Soup
Brisket *(doubled)*
Asian Noodle-Rice Casserole
Sugar Snap Peas with Cashews *(doubled)*
Orange Glazed Carrots *(doubled)*
Challah (Egg Bread) *(two loaves)*
Blender Pecan Pie
Blueberry Pie

Vegetarian Dinner I
Serves 4
Tomato and Corn Soup
Lentil and Rice Casserole
Tossed Green Salad
Cherry Pie

Vegetarian Dinner II
Serves 4
Tortellini
  with Broccoli and Artichokes
Tossed Green Salad
Crusty Bread
The Perfect Brownie

Vegetarian Dinner III
Serves 4
Spinach, Mushroom, and Tofu Soup
Cold Bean and Artichoke Salad
  (on Plate of Salad Greens)
Layered Cookie Bars

Vegetarian Dinner IV
Serves 4
Grilled Portobello Mushrooms
Nutty Thai Noodles
Spinach with Lemon and Pepper
  (doubled)
Pineapple Cake

Special Occasion Brunch I
Serves 12
Egg Casserole with Lox and Onions
Blintz Casserole
Bagels with Cream Cheese
Cut-up Fresh Fruit

Menus

Special Occasion Brunch II
Serves 12
Blintz Casserole
Light and Fluffy Cheesy Eggs *(doubled)*
Bagels with Cream Cheese
Cut-up Fresh Fruit

Brunch I
Serves 6
Egg Casserole
Cinnamon Raisin Bread
Grits with Cream *(doubled)*
Cut-up Fresh Fruit

Brunch II
Serves 6
Overnight Blueberry French Toast
Cheesy Potato Skillet *(doubled)*
Cut-up Fresh Fruit

Brunch III
Serves 6
Light and Fluffy Cheesy Eggs
Pecan Biscuit Ring
Hot Fruit Compote

Brunch IV
Serves 6
Anytime Quiche
Blintz Casserole
One Pot Banana Bread
Tossed Green Salad

Recipe Index

Recipe Index continued

Recipe Index continued

Recipe Index continued

Recipe Index continued

Recipe Index continued

Recipe Index continued

Reference Lists

Inspiration

Brokaw, Meredith and Gilbar, Annie. <u>The Penny Whistle Birthday Party Book</u>. New York: Simon and Schuster/ Fireside, 1992.

Dupree, Nathalie. <u>Everyday Meals From a Well-Stocked Pantry</u>. New York: Clarkson N. Potter, Inc., member of the Crown Publishing Group, 1995.

Dupree, Nathalie. <u>New Southern Cooking</u>. New York: Alfred A. Knopf, 1987.

Eisenberg, Arlene; Murkoff, Heidi E.; and Hathaway, B.S.N., Sandee E. <u>What to Expect the First Year.</u> New York: Workman Publishing, 1989.

Haughton, Natalie Hartanov. <u>The Best Slow Cooker Cookbook Ever</u>. New York: Harper Collins, 1995.

Hoffman, Mable. <u>Healthy Crockery Cookery</u>. New York: The Berkley Publishing Group, a member of Penguin Putnam, Inc., 1998.

Iovine, Vickie. <u>The Girlfriend's Guide to Surviving the First Year of Motherhood.</u> New York: a Pedigree Book published by The Berkley Publishing Group, a member of Penguin Putnam, Inc., 1997.

Lansky, Vicky. <u>Birthday Parties: Best Tips and Ideas</u> (third expanded edition). Minnetonka, MN: Book Peddlers, 1995.

Rombauer, Irma S.; Rombauer Becker, Marion; and Becker, Ethan. <u>The All New All Purpose Joy of Cooking</u>. New York: Scribner, 1997.

Rosso, Julie and Lukins, Sheila. <u>The New Basics Cookbook</u>. New York: Workman Publishing, 1989.

Rosso, Julie and Lukins, Sheila. <u>The Silver Palate Cookbook</u>. New York: Workman Publishing, 1982.

Notes

Notes

Notes

Notes

Notes

Notes

BILL TO: *(Credit Card Billing Address)*

NAME   *PLEASE PRINT*

ADDRESS

CITY   STATE   ZIP

DAYTIME PHONE *(Required for Shipment)*

SHIP TO: *(If different than bill to)*

NAME   *PLEASE PRINT*

ADDRESS

CITY   STATE   ZIP

DAYTIME PHONE *(Required for Shipment)*

Make Checks Payable to: **Empire Press**

Mail to: **Empire Press**
    660 Spindlewick Drive, Atlanta, GA 30350

ACCEPTED METHODS OF PAYMENT
Credit Cards: Visa, Mastercard, Discover, American Express
Check: Money Order, Cashier's check or personal check*
Sorry, no COD's
If paying with a personal check, please allow ten days from our receipt of check to date of shipment from our warehouse. Check must clear bank before order is processed. Name, address, and account number must be imprinted on check; no counter checks accepted.

Please send me _____ copies of
The One-Armed Cook @ $24.95 each

Georgia Residents add
7% state tax @ $1.76 each

Shipping and Handling @ 5.95 each

TOTAL

❑ Money Order   ❑ Cashier's Check   ❑ Personal Check*
❑ Visa   ❑ MasterCard   ❑ Discover   ❑ American Express

Method of Payment EXPIRATION DATE _____

NAME AS IT APPEARS ON CARD

AUTHORIZED SIGNATURE

Credit Card Orders call 1-866-936-7473 Or Fax this Order Form to 770-393-1288 Or order online at www.theonearmedcook.com

---

BILL TO: *(Credit Card Billing Address)*

NAME   *PLEASE PRINT*

ADDRESS

CITY   STATE   ZIP

DAYTIME PHONE *(Required for Shipment)*

SHIP TO: *(If different than bill to)*

NAME   *PLEASE PRINT*

ADDRESS

CITY   STATE   ZIP

DAYTIME PHONE *(Required for Shipment)*

Make Checks Payable to: **Empire Press**

Mail to: **Empire Press**
    660 Spindlewick Drive, Atlanta, GA 30350

ACCEPTED METHODS OF PAYMENT
Credit Cards: Visa, Mastercard, Discover, American Express
Check: Money Order, Cashier's check or personal check*
Sorry, no COD's
If paying with a personal check, please allow ten days from our receipt of check to date of shipment from our warehouse. Check must clear bank before order is processed. Name, address, and account number must be imprinted on check; no counter checks accepted.

Please send me _____ copies of
The One-Armed Cook @ $24.95 each

Georgia Residents add
7% state tax @ $1.76 each

Shipping and Handling @ 5.95 each

TOTAL

❑ Money Order   ❑ Cashier's Check   ❑ Personal Check*
❑ Visa   ❑ MasterCard   ❑ Discover   ❑ American Express

Method of Payment EXPIRATION DATE _____

NAME AS IT APPEARS ON CARD

AUTHORIZED SIGNATURE

Credit Card Orders call 1-866-936-7473 Or Fax this Order Form to 770-393-1288 Or order online at www.theonearmedcook.com